DISCARD

S0-BOJ-339

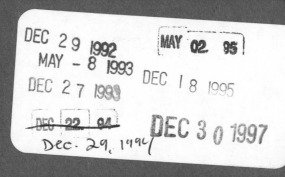

DEC 29 1992   MAY 02 95
  MAY - 8 1993 DEC 18 1995
DEC 27 1993
  DEC 22 94   DEC 30 1997
  Dec. 29, 1994

COPY 17

j394   **MILLEN, Nina**
M   *Children's festivals from many lands.* Illus. by Janet
        Smalley. New York, Friendship [c.1964] 191p. illus.
                    3.95

RELATED   *1. Festivals*
BOOKS IN   Tells of 165 festivals held during the year throughout the
CATALOG   world.
UNDER

                              Title. O 68

51556   4

Children's Festivals from Many Lands

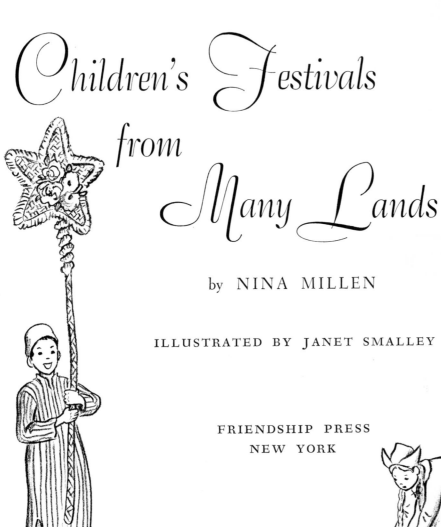

Children's Festivals from Many Lands

by NINA MILLEN

ILLUSTRATED BY JANET SMALLEY

FRIENDSHIP PRESS
NEW YORK

LIBRARY OF CONGRESS CATALOG CARD NUMBER: 64-14664

COPYRIGHT © 1964 BY FRIENDSHIP PRESS, INC.
PRINTED IN THE UNITED STATES OF AMERICA

Allen Park Public Library
8100 Allen Road
Allen Park, Mich. 48101

$\mathcal{C}$ontents

6 : *Contents*

3. ASIA

FOLK FESTIVALS

CHRISTIAN FESTIVALS

FOLK FESTIVALS

CHRISTIAN FESTIVALS

5. NORTH AMERICA

FOLK FESTIVALS

CHRISTIAN FESTIVALS

6. SOUTH AMERICA

FOLK FESTIVALS

CHRISTIAN FESTIVALS

7. PACIFIC LANDS 168

FOLK FESTIVALS

CHRISTIAN FESTIVALS

8. FESTIVAL TIME WITH CHILDREN 173

INDEX 185

Children's Festivals from Many Lands

: 1 :

Festival Days

The observance of a festival has a universal appeal to the heart of man. In the procession of days through which he passes, year after year, certain ones are set apart for their special significance. He strives to honor these days by carrying out certain traditional rites, and he celebrates them with gaiety, feasting, and fellowship.

In almost every country and among almost every people of the world, the keeping of festivals is part of the cultural pattern. So deeply is the custom imbedded in the cultures that, though it may be interrupted as wars come and go, famines lay waste the land, or pestilence destroys much of the population, once the disturbance has passed, the people return to their old ways, and the festivals they knew in childhood are celebrated once more. The festivals usually have their roots in the far past and some of the customs attending them arise from religious beliefs now long forgotten.

Certain times of the year and certain occasions seem to awaken mankind to a spirit of celebration. Such occasions are the coming of spring, the gathering of the harvest, and the arrival of the new year. Such festivals are celebrated in a variety of ways among a great many different peoples. Yet they have a common thread in their outpouring of the human spirit and the oneness of expressing and preserving a common heritage.

The springtime festivals are marked by joy and hope and expectation; the harvest celebrations, by thanksgiving and contentment. The time of the New Year festival varies from place to place, since different cultures have different beliefs as to when the new year actually begins. But there is a certain similarity in the ideas connected with the New Year celebration. The days of the old year, with their trials and sorrows, their mistakes and disappointments, are to be forgotten. In East Asia, at the close of the old year, debts are paid or forgiven, old quarrels patched up, and old clothes put away in preparation for the new year. Almost everywhere the wearing of new clothes, the enjoying of newly prepared food, the making of resolutions for improved behavior in the days ahead, the seeking of good fortune, and similar customs, are symbolic of the hope that with the new year a better time is dawning. Off with the old, on with the new!

Patriotic festivals are joyous events in many countries. They celebrate important happenings in the development of the country toward independent nationhood—such as the success of a revolutionary movement, the winning of an important battle, the launching of a new type of government. In this volume, however, patriotic festivals are not included because of lack of space. The focus of our selection is entirely on the basis of *folk festivals and Christian festivals that are enjoyed by children and their families.*

The majority of folk and Christian festivals are celebrated by the

whole family—father, mother, children, and relatives. A few festivals, however, are specifically for children, although the parents usually play a major role in them as well.

Some countries and cultures seem to be abloom with colorful festivals for children and delightful ways of celebrating them. Such a country is Japan, with its Girls' Day and Boys' Day, its New Year festival, its moon viewing and flower viewing parties.

The Latin American countries have their gay *fiesta* days, which mark a number of special occasions with gaiety and feasting. North America celebrates beloved special days, with birthday parties, Valentine's Day surprises, May Day baskets, Hallowe'en tricks and treats, Thanksgiving dinners, and all the merry festivities of Christmas and the New Year.

But it is especially important to note that wherever the Christian gospel has gone, it has taken with it the celebration of Christian festivals, particularly those of Christmas and Easter. In many places the new Christians and the young churches have been content to celebrate these festivals in the ways they have been taught by the missionaries. In other places the people have taken the Christmas and Easter festivals to themselves, adapted and changed them to fit their culture, and brought forth something new and fresh and different. The Christian customs included in this book are mainly those which are culturally indigenous and thus have about them that touch of the new and different.

In looking over the festival descriptions, one is struck by certain similarities in the customs of countries that are far apart in the geographical sense. Bonfires are built on Bonfire Day (Guy Fawkes Day) in England; on Midsummer Day in Scandinavia; on Saint John's Day in Brazil, and other places. In several lands the children gather wood for the fires, and

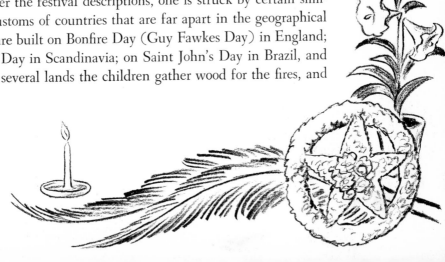

in others there is a custom of people jumping over the blazing fire to insure good luck. Another common custom is that of boys and girls going about from house to house to ask for cakes or fruit or candy or money as at the New Year in Korea and at Christmas in Ghana, on Candy Holiday in Turkey and on Hallowe'en in Scotland and Canada and the United States.

The material in this book is, with few exceptions, entirely *original*. Some of the material here exists in no other collection. The descriptions of the festivals have been collected almost entirely from missionaries, nationals, and residents, who know the country and people about which they are writing and whose names are signed to their contributions.

: 2 :

Africa

FOLK FESTIVALS

Angola

THE FEAST OF NGANJA

Every year when the harvest is ripe in Angola—that is, in the month of April—the children from about eight years to twelve invite each other saying, "On Monday (or another day) we will eat the feast of *Nganja*."

On the day named, they all go out to their family fields, each to his own, to gather some fresh ripe corn. Later they meet in a beautiful part of the woods near a little stream. In small groups, they light fires and roast corn on the cob. While they are roasting the corn or starting to eat it they have to be always on the watch, because someone may suddenly come to rob them of the corn. For, in the twinkling of an eye, someone jumps up, leaves his fire and corn, and rushes to grab the corn of another group. That is where the fun of this feast lies, in the excitement of mutual robbing and plundering. The children run and shout and laugh, although some are sad because they lose their ears of roasted corn and gain none.

After a day of fun, the Feast of *Nganja* ends. And before the sun sinks they all run home to the village. Few eat anything more for supper that night.—*Jacob Cavita Evambi*

THE FEAST OF OKAMBONDONDO

This feast may be held several times in the year, usually during the months of February, March, and April, the harvest months in Angola. The children invite all of their own age or group saying, "On such and such a day we will have *Okambondondo*." Often those from six years to ten hold their feast in one place, and those from eleven to fifteen in another. And often those from sixteen up have a feast of their own.

The feast lasts all night. The girls bring cornmeal and corn and beans, and the boys bring dried fish or meat. The children borrow the big pots from the owner of the kitchen where they plan to hold the feast. In the evening, they play games and tell folk stories. Then the boys go to sleep in their house, and the girls sleep in their kitchen. But about one or two o'clock in the morning, the girls get up and make the cornmeal mush, and prepare the cracked corn porridge, and the bean and meat relish. They run to waken the boys and call them to the feast in the kitchen. They all eat together and then go to the village common to play and sing. They sing a special song, "We have eaten our *Okambondondo* in the night." One group sings the first five words, and the others add "in the night." When the first streaks of dawn show they get together all the food they have left and carry it to their own homes for their parents to taste of the feast. Tired children? Of course! But they are allowed to sleep late the next day.—*Jacob Cavita Evambi*

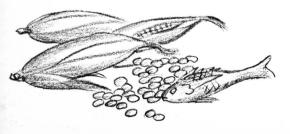

THE FEAST OF KAPESI

When the busy planting time in Angola is over and the work is light, little girls and older girls and even women name a day, and on that day they all go to some prearranged place near a stream. They take various kinds of food with them and spend the day there. The main feature of this feast is that the girls make baskets all day long from morning until evening when they return to the village. While the food is cooking in the pots, they work at their baskets until it is time to eat, and after they have eaten, they work again on their baskets. And as they work, the girls sing and tell stories. No boys are invited to this feast, but sometimes saucy little fellows go out to where the girls are in order to taste the food they have. When the sun has gone down and darkness begins to fall, the girls all go home, singing songs as they go to their houses in the village.
—*Jacob Cavita Evambi*

Congo

LEOPARD PANTOMIME

The leopard pantomime may be done at any time, but it is most effective around a campfire at night. It may form part of the entertainment at any festival. A small boy wears the mask of a leopard and is draped with a leopard skin. He comes stealthily forward, imitating a leopard. He pretends to hear a sound and darts back into the forest, then

comes forward again, cautiously. Suddenly he staggers, pretending to be wounded by an arrow or a spear. He struggles and falls to the ground as if dead.

African boys love to imitate various animals in this way and are very dramatic about it.—*Ruth Dickey*

HARVEST FESTIVAL

At the close of the dry season, which lasts from June to September in the Congo, and just before the rains come, the villagers celebrate the hope of harvest festival. The women have made their gardens and everyone hopes for a good harvest. The festival's purpose is to assure a good harvest.

The village people arm themselves with dried gourds for rattles. A drummer is hired for the occasion, and he sits in the center of an open space and beats upon his tom-tom. The people form circles and move slowly around the drummer, shaking their rattles (made of dried gourds with pebbles or seeds inside) and chanting, as they keep time with the drum with stamping feet and clapping hands. The children form their own circles in the center near the drummer, keeping time with hands and feet. At this time the little girls often wear special necklaces of seeds threaded on a string.—*Ruth Dickey*

Egypt

SMELL THE BREEZES

Smell the Breezes, *Shem al Neseem,* is an all-Egyptian festival and people of all religions in the country celebrate it. Its origin is lost in antiquity, but it is definitely a welcome to spring. Since the time of the celebration depends upon the spring equinox, it always falls on the Monday following the Eastern Easter.

The whole day is a holiday, but the actual celebration takes place in the early morning. Everyone who is able— man, woman, and child—gets up before dawn and hastens out into the fields and lanes, or into the city parks, to enjoy the sweet smell of spring. There is no lying in bed for one who would celebrate *Shem al Neseem.*

At break of day the sound of joyous people can be heard on every street. Fragrant flowers and pungent herbs are prized. A red rose with a sprig of mint is to be seen in the hand of almost every holiday maker.

Every little girl wants a bright new frock for this glad morning. If she is a village girl, her new red or green or blue dress will fall full and straight from a yoke, ending in a ruffle about her ankles. If she is a city girl, her dress will be pretty and bright but not distinctly Egyptian.

Little brother's outfit is also determined by where he lives. The village boy will have a new striped garment, not unlike a loose nightshirt, that reaches to his feet. His city cousin may be decked out in new shirt and shorts, or perhaps in a new pajama suit—the brighter the stripes, the better.

A picnic breakfast is the order of the day. Family groups can be seen in any open place, eating bread, cheese, fish, and some salad vegetable; and always dried fish, kidney beans, and green onions. Sometimes the family picnics are held on the beach or at an oasis or pyramid. Eggs, the symbol of spring, are essential, and, of course, the shells must be colored. Village women in their black draped garments may be seen in every marketplace beside baskets piled high with eggs dyed in brilliant hues of scarlet, purple, green, or gold.

The morning's outing over, the crowds trudge wearily homeward. Spring has been officially welcomed, and everyone is happy.—*Mrs. H. S. Hutchison*[1]

Ethiopia

NEW YEAR'S EVE

In Ethiopia the new year comes in the first six days of our September. Its celebration resembles somewhat the old custom of giving May Day baskets, in which flowers and sweets are exchanged between friends.

On August 31, as the sun sets in its gorgeous coloring over the mountains to the west of Ethiopia, the children and some young people gather in front of their houses, wearing white clothes and carrying in their hands as many flowers as they have been able to beg from their friends and neighbors. It is a picturesque sight. Then, as the evening falls, they begin to make the rounds of the houses, knocking on the doors. After receiving permission to enter, they sing a little song, hand the head of the house and his wife one of their tiny bouquets, and stand waiting.

They are expecting the gift they know will come from most of the houses. Sometimes it is a two-cent piece; sometimes a cooky or a piece

[1] For a story based on this festival, see *Deedee's Holiday,* by Jeanette Perkins Brown. Friendship Press.

of candy. Or it may be a vegetable or a lime, something that is found in the household supplies and can easily be given away.

The chorus of soft voices giving thanks, *"Wakiyo se fakenee"* (God also give to you) melts away on the evening air, and the knocking and the songs begin at the gate next door. Until the night falls or there is no one else from whom to beg, the bands of children roam about. Then they run back to their homes and display to their parents the gifts that they have received during the evening.—*Mrs. Duncan C. Henry*

Ghana

YAM FESTIVAL

This is a yearly children's festival which is held by the children of Agona district, in Ghana, just as the rainy season comes to a close. It is generally held in the first and second weeks of the month of August, when the food crops on the farms begin to mature, the fresh yams and cocoyams are ready for harvest, and dry maize is in abundance. Garden vegetables such as okra and beans are ripe, and everyone begins to forget about the hungry days of the past few months.

August is also the month in which grownups in the town celebrate the Yam Festival, which is known as the "To Hoot at Famine." Fresh yams can now be dug and brought home carried on the heads of the women gardeners. Every farm woman takes pride in bringing home for this festival fully matured yams so that she may be known as the best farmer of the town.

The adult festival goes on with its rituals and other customary performances for one week, but the children may prolong theirs for two weeks. For the festival the children under twelve or thirteen years collect meat and other foodstuffs from their houses and gather together in an open place, where the girls begin to cook the food. Several groups of children may celebrate this festival in different areas. When the food is

ready, the girls invite their little brothers, cousins, and friends to come and dine with them.

After this repast, they play games and "make-believe." Two popular boys' games are somersault and throw-and-catch. For somersaulting a thick and solid coconut palm branch is cut and fixed into a hilly ground. The girls stand by and cheer the best performers. *Odo,* throw-and-catch, is another exciting game. A fairly thick tassel is made of palm leaves, with the midribs removed. The boys divide into two sides. The tassel is thrown into the air, and while it is falling back, the players stand with loops made of fiber to catch it. Whoever catches it gains a point for his group.

The girls also divide into two sides and play a game in which a pair of players, one from each side, leap up, each stretching a leg forward at the same time. If the players stretch out different legs, as a left and a right, one side counts a point. If they stretch out the same leg, as right-right or left-left, the other side gets a point. Boys have a similar game, but they throw out their arms instead of their legs and they keep time by clapping instead of jumping.—*J. D. Okae*

Nigeria

ZOLLA FESTIVAL

The *Zolla* festival is held in the latter part of October at the time of the new moon and lasts from five to seven days. It celebrates the in-gathering of the harvest and the starting of a new year for the people of the Wurkum tribes of Northern Nigeria.

It is celebrated by old and young and is the time when everyone gets a new outfit of clothing. The boys prefer long trousers and either white or colored sport shirts. The girls have brilliantly figured wrap-around dresses and turbans. Beads are much in evidence.

On the afternoon of the day appointed, near sundown, all put on their new clothes and go out in the yard and face the west. Father heads the line, standing with spear, bow and arrows in his hands. The older sons have their spears also. The family stands in a line to the left of the father. As the sun sinks in the west all must be *very* quiet—not a move, not a whisper. Even the dogs sense the tension and sit with eyes on their masters.

An appointed elder of the village stands on a high place above the village and faces the east. The quiet is intense! They wait! Far to the east is heard a shout, the next village to the west of it taking up the cry. Nearer and nearer—from village to village. At last the elder raises his arms and shouts. Bedlam breaks loose. Father turns from a living statue to a dancing maniac for a few minutes. The children shout, beat on tins or drums, and dance with joy. The *Zolla* is here! After a few minutes of shouting, the food will be ready. After eating it, all will go to the village square to dance by the light of bonfires and torches. Men and women dance separately. The smaller children play games, the others trying to imitate the intricate, rhythmic shoulder muscle jerks and stomping feet of the older ones in the dance.

The following days are spent in visiting friends and getting refreshments and then dancing at night. The special food served at this time is *Zolla* bread made of guinea corn or maize flour cooked to a thick mush and then fried in peanut oil.—*Mrs. D'Alta Armold*

Sierra Leone

THE NEW YEAR FESTIVAL

San Khuda is one of the traditional festivals observed by the Mandingo tribe of Sierra Leone. The New Year festival comes at seed-sowing time, in late April or early May, during the full moon. It lasts for a day and a half. The festival falls at the close of the dry season, when high temperatures have evaporated streams and rivers, scorched the grass, and stopped most plant growth. The wet season is beginning, when the flowing of the rivers, the growing of plants, and greenness of grass renews the life. For centuries the people have believed that water is the source of life to all living things and that it loses its power through use. Hence, they believe that an act of God takes the old water away, as the old year ends, and that this miracle takes place at sunset in the last day of the closing year. Therefore the people must give thanks and rejoice.

The celebration is observed by young and old. On the eve of the festival, the families clean their houses, sweep their yards, and get their troughs and other utensils ready to receive the New Year's water. Some families observe the day with feasting. But it is water that is most important to everyone. Each household makes sure there is enough of it for drinking, cooking, and washing.

The children's part comes early on New Year's Eve. A number of children, with their mothers, start folk singing and dancing at some central place of the town or village, accompanied by music from drums or flutes. Other children gather there with water buckets. At the leader's signal, everyone goes, singing, to the public spring or river.

At the spring the buckets are filled with water, and the group is ready to return to town carrying water on their heads and palm branches in their hands, and singing in serious mood the New Year song:

The old year has gone by, The new year has come in!
The old water is taken out, The new water is brought in!
At the coming of a new year, Some may live, others will die.

The tribe, including the children, go from house to house, dipping the palm branches into the water and sprinkling everything they wish to bless—people, doorsteps, animals, and houses. Older people then come out of doors with gifts to receive the blessing. After all this, they return to the spring in family groups to bring the water needed for each household. Some of the children go back and forth three times to get the water required. With so much activity interspersed with laughter and glee, no one seems to notice the time, and each child goes to bed tired, happy, and blessed by the New Year.—*Sylmadi E. Warratie*

CHRISTIAN FESTIVALS

Congo

CHRISTMAS

The singing of carols and the dramatization of the Christmas story mark the festive season among the Christians in the Congo villages. A palm branch shelter is made for the Holy Family and decorated with flowers. When it is time for the play to begin, the drum beats out the call "Come, see, come, see." Visitors are greeted with a cheery "*Yo, yo! Yo, yo!*"

The whole village may take part in the drama, men and women lining up before the "tax collectors" at the start. Joseph and Mary appear and are told there is no room in any house for them. They go to the palm branch shelter. A cradle is there with a real baby in it. Soon shepherds appear with some live goats and they make their bows to the little family. Then come the Wise Men, wearing costumes of artistically twisted scarfs of bright colors and carrying black native pots and gourds for their

gifts of gold and perfume for the baby. Carols are sung as the climax, and all who know them join in.

Egypt

CHRISTMAS AND EASTER

In Egypt, Christmas is known as the "little feast" and Easter as the "big feast." Both are widely celebrated by all Christian groups. Many of the foreigners in the country belong either to the Roman Catholic or the Greek Orthodox Church. The largest group of Egyptian Christians belong to the ancient Coptic Church. Greek and Coptic Christians follow the Old Calendar and thus celebrate Christmas on January 6, and Easter a week later than the Western Easter. The Evangelical Church, as the Protestant Church is called in Egypt, follows the festival customs of the Coptic Church to a large extent. Christmas and Easter celebrations, however, are tinged with Western influence—due largely to mission school festivities.

New clothes for a holiday and special foods mark all Egyptian feasts, whether Muslim or Christian. (Gift giving is a Western mode of celebrating.) Special sweet cakes mark both the Christian feasts and the big Muslim feast following the Ramadan fast.—*Mrs. H. S. Hutchison*

PALM SUNDAY

For the Egyptian Christian child, no other religious festival can overshadow the excitement of Palm Sunday. The service in the Coptic Christian Church seems irreverently noisy to the Western onlooker, but actually it is joyous and festive.

For a day or two beforehand, Coptic families are busy plaiting their palm branches. The small, tender, white fronds are stripped from the inside of the palm leaves, then woven or braided into intricate patterns. You may see a shield, an anchor, a triangle, and many other shapes. Some are mounted on long stems and often there is a tassel at the top. Usually they are decorated with flowers—the favorite being red roses but with other blooms being used. A sweet scent and a bright color are both important. Many a small child, and even older school children, will be seen carrying palm creations taller than themselves.

Having made the palm branches for the festive day, the children, accompanied by their parents, carry them to church on Palm Sunday. This is the particular role of children in the festival. Dressed in their best, they attend church in great numbers on Palm Sunday. Formerly the service was entirely in the ancient Coptic language, which was not understood by the people, but now the story of the triumphal entry of our Lord is always read in Arabic, their native language.

At last the moment comes for which all have waited! The priest comes forth with holy water to sprinkle, and so to bless, the palm branches. Everyone presses forward to get his branch sprinkled. Sometimes the priest ends by throwing the water at the crowd to reach all the branches.

Satisfied, the people make their way homeward. The precious palm branch is then hung on the wall to bring blessing to the house until another year rolls around to a new Palm Sunday.—*Mrs. H. S. Hutchison*

Ethiopia

CHRISTMAS GAME

In many parts of Ethiopia very little preparation or excitement precedes Christmas Day, as the common people know so very little of what Christmas means. But there is one custom, said to have come from the Christmas story, that has penetrated even the remote parts of the country—the playing of the *Ko-lee* game.

Sometime during the last part of November each boy goes into the nearby forest and hunts for a stick of a very special kind. It must be a small sapling with heavy knobby roots, or a branch that has a sort of knobby knuckle at its joining to the tree. This sapling is uprooted, or the branch gently cut with the knuckle attached to the stick, and then carried carefully home to begin a drying process. As it dries, various things must be done to it. First, a rough stone—or better still, a broken piece of glass—must be used to scrape the bark from the sapling or branch. The root is also scraped and made into a head something like the head of a golf club. And wax or oil is worked into the grain of the wood so that it will not crack and break.

Meanwhile another small piece of knobby wood is cut and roughly scraped into the shape of a ball. It really never attains the roundness of a ball, but it takes the place of one.

During the last four or five weeks before Christmas, the boys and younger men begin to play with the sticks and the wooden balls on any open field or playground that may be near their homes. The rules are somewhat like those used in ground hockey. The game is played faster and more furiously as Christmas Day nears. Why do they play it? What is its meaning? It was some years before we found one who could explain it to us. Then it came as a surprise!

Had we never heard of the shepherd boys and men who were watching the sheep on the night Jesus was born? Well, they were playing this game as they watched their sheep, and so as Christmas nears, the boys and men must play this in memory of those shepherds to whom was given the first news of the coming of the Christ. Not very many of those who play the game today know the source of the story, but that is the meaning of the Christmas *Ko-lee* game of Ethiopia.—*Mrs. Duncan C. Henry*

Ghana

CHRISTMAS

Christmas is a time of great joy for all Christians. But children especially rejoice in it. Here in Ghana the festival continues for eight days, the children making great merriment during the holiday.

Every year on the twenty-fifth of December Ghanaian children are given new clothes and other gifts by their parents and relatives. Early in the morning the children help their mothers in the kitchen, and after taking a bath, eat their early meal, perhaps mashed yams cooked with eggs and palm oil.

The church bells ring three different times during the morning of the twenty-fifth. On the third ringing, which is usually at ten o'clock, the children put on their best clothes and go to church to hear the story of the birth of Jesus and also to sing carols. After the service they return home.

Usually fowl, but sometimes sheep or goats, are killed for the Christmas meal. Yam is pounded into *fufu,* and a highly flavored and delicious soup is prepared with meat and eggs. After these sumptuous dishes have been eaten, the children's festival begins.

In every street in the town one finds groups or bands of children of various ages, boys and girls either separately or together, moving happily from house to house. At the door of every house to which they come, one hears them sing their original songs. *"Buronya 'du oo, afe ato yen bio!"* (It is Christmas, a new year is come!) *Papa ee (Mamma ee), yeaba wo fie-ee-ee, yeaba wo fie,"* ("Father [or mother], we have come to your house.") And so on.

If a father or a mother or any grown-up person in any of the houses visited gives some presents to the children, they sing as an appreciation for the gift this song: *"Papa ee (Mamma ee), wo yam ye, Ada kye, ade kye a, wo yam ye,"* ("Father [or mother], you are kind. You will continue to be kind.")

If, however, the householders are unable to give any presents to the children because several other children have already visited them, the words may be altered to: *"Papa ee (Mamma ee), wo yam mô, Ade kye, ade kye a, wo yam mô,"* ("Father [or mother], you are unkind. You will continue to be unkind.") Sometimes, the children will not sing but will greet the people in the houses, saying: *"Papa (Mamma), yebesan wo afe!"* ("Father [or mother], we come to wish you a merry Christmas!")

The children continue their house-to-house visits every day for eight days. Sometimes, instead of singing, they make some homemade trumpets with pawpaw stalks and the membranous spider's web. They make all sorts of unusual sounds with these trumpets with a view to asking for presents from the householders.—*J. D. Okae*

CHILDREN'S DAY

This day is celebrated by children under sixteen. It comes once a year on the Sunday set aside for it. On that day the children of both Christian and non-Christian families are allowed to hold their Sunday worship in the big church, instead of outside under a shady tree. Worshiping in the sanctuary gives them the feeling that they will one day be members there.

The children put on their best clothes and march in a procession through the streets of the town, singing and rejoicing as they make their way to the church. Sometimes there is a band that plays as they march.

The children are led into the church by a young man or woman and the service that day is conducted by a teacher. Hymns and songs are sung; prayers with responses are offered by children and adults; Bible verses are read, and Bible passages recited by boys and girls of various age groups. The children give their offering, which is usually money they have obtained by selling something they have grown or by doing work for which they were paid. This offering is used for God's work in other places.

When the service is over, the children march to their usual meeting place before they go home. In the evening they meet again and sing joyful Christian songs until the sun goes down.—*J. D. Okae*

Natal, South Africa

CHRISTMAS

In our part of Africa, Christmas comes in summer instead of winter. In one village of Zulu people, the Christians have a Christmas tree not of fir but of gum (eucalyptus). Its long slender branches are trimmed with tinsel and shiny ornaments. On Christmas morning the Christians go to the church service in the village. The older women sit on the left, the older men on the right, and the young people and children fill the center benches.

The day after Christmas, the Christians gather around the tree. The young people sing the songs they have learned and between songs they distribute gifts. Often a person will receive a chicken feather or a pineapple leaf, which means that a chicken or a pineapple will be given when it is grown.

In the evening at sunset time, there is a picnic on the lawn, and everyone enjoys the end of a happy day.—*Mary A. Beals*

Nigeria

CHRISTMAS IN WURKUMLAND

In northeastern Nigeria are people of the Kulung and Pero tribes, known collectively as the Wurkum people.

The day before Christmas, the Christians who own lanterns make sure they have an adequate supply of kerosene, for after dark they take turns sitting in a group, their small lanterns providing the light as they sing hymns and carols from dark until the first streaks of dawn appear in the sky. Those who do not participate in the singing may be awakened by songs at any time throughout the night, and because of the singing they are reminded immediately that it is Christmas Eve or Christmas morning.

Just as the light of Christmas Day is appearing in the sky, the bell at the mission is rung and the singers and all the other Christians—men, women, and children—gather inside the church for a very short worship service. They then divide into groups and go out in different directions to the various villages. Along the way, each group makes numerous stops. At each stopping place, Christmas songs are sung and then one of

the group tells the Christmas story to all who have gathered to hear—telling why we have Christmas, what Christmas means, why Christ came into the world, what he has done for each one, and why we love him, worship him, and live for him. Thus, on each early Christmas morning the gospel is presented along the road to all who will listen. After the singing of another carol, the group moves on to another place. At nightfall, the groups return to their homes, happy and ready for food.

In the late morning or early afternoon, the Christians from the outlying villages come in, and a Christmas church service is held. After this there is a social period on the mission compound—the playing of games and a general good time, followed by a feast for all who have gathered.

Gift giving as known in the United States is not practiced. A few eggs or a small amount of guinea corn may be given by one person to another, but that is about the extent of it.—*Lucy Rowe*

EASTER

Good Friday is celebrated in some sections by a service and a planting of seed in the earth in memory of Christ's burial. Everyone plants a seed or two. This is a very impressive service. Easter Sunday is celebrated by a big church service. It is a time of rejoicing with singing throughout the day.—*Mrs. D'Alta Armold*

Portuguese East Africa—Mozambique

BLESSING OF SEEDS AND TOOLS

As the planting season starts, the Christian families at Kambine, Mozambique, come to the church for a short service of worship. They bring with them the seeds and the tools they will use in planting. The women and girls, who do the majority of the garden work, lay their baskets of seeds and their hoes on the altar, while the first line of the

planting song (see below) is chanted by the leader, followed by the entire group singing the rest of the verses. The teacher then talks about planting the seeds in the right way and how all must work to make the gardens grow.

Seeds and tools are left on the altar of the church for the night. At sunrise, the workers return and sing the last verse. Then they pick up the seeds and hoes and go out to start work on their gardens, often singing as they go, "The man who is happy is the one who digs." In the song they cover the activities of planting, tending the crop, and getting a good harvest.

1. Seeds we bring, Lord to thee,
   Wilt thou bless them, O Lord.
2. Hoes we bring, Lord to thee,
   Wilt thou bless them, O Lord.
3. Hands we bring, Lord to thee,
   Wilt thou bless them, O Lord.
4. Ourselves we bring, Lord to thee,
   Wilt thou bless us, O Lord.

—From *Child Guidance in Christian Living*, General Board of Education of the Methodist Church. Copyright, 1945. Used by permission. Music of song to be found in *The Whole World Singing*, 1950, Friendship Press.

Southern Rhodesia

CHRISTMAS

In the southeastern corner of Southern Rhodesia among the brown-skinned Shangaans tribe, *Kisimusi,* or Christmas, is a festival taken over from the Europeans but celebrated with particular African flavor. The twenty-fifth of December, coming in early summer, is usually a hot, and often a rainy, day. Families begin preparations some days or weeks in advance, depending upon financial circumstances. Girls and boys get as excited as North American children do over the prospects of a big feast and new clothes.

If the father can afford it he may get gay scarves or bright-colored dresses or sweaters for his little girls, bright-colored shirts and shorts, or perhaps shoes, for his little boys, and a silk dress for his wife. Father also gets loaves of bread, jam, tea, and sugar. Then on Christmas Day the family and friends have their feast.

In the Christian village home, the parents do their best to prepare as large a feast as possible, give gifts of clothing to their children, and candy to friends' children. Christmas Day begins with attendance at the early morning church service. The children usually participate in a song which they have practiced especially for this day.

Sometimes a feast is held for all the people of the church. The mothers then take turns preparing the church feast, so that others can attend the service. Everyone, old and young, streams from the church toward the home where the feast is being prepared, and those who are not helping sit down under a shady tree and wait to be served. There will be

fresh roast ox or goat, if the village is prosperous, cornmeal porridge (very stiff), bread, jam, tea, and sugar. The men and boys are served first, then the women and girls. The church does not invite outsiders, but no one who passes by is turned away.

After everyone is satisfied, all sit back and relax, singing gospel songs, followed by a time of devotions. If there are many non-Christians present, the local preacher will give an evangelistic sermon with the hopes of winning them to God. The herd boys go dancing back to their herding nearby, the girls play their games around the fires until the sun begins to sink in the west, and Christmas is over.—*Florence A. Sayre*

EASTER

Among the Shangaans of southeastern Rhodesia, where the gospel has been preached to this generation only, Easter customs are not as yet strongly established. In a community with a lively church, however, the young people go out long before dawn, singing the Easter hymns in the non-Christian villages, so that they can reach many villages before it becomes hot, as March is summertime here. They urge the people to come to the Easter service at the church. The church program is not elaborate, but there is usually much singing, and often there will be a visiting preacher. A large number of non-Christians often respond to the invitation, so the church is usually filled to capacity.

Usually several small churches join together on Easter Sunday. An important part of the service is the singing of the many lovely Easter hymns translated into their African dialect.—*Florence A. Sayre*

West Africa—Cameroun

THANKSGIVING

The Christians in Cameroun celebrate their Thanksgiving Day, *Evamelunga,* on September 8. On that morning, the little chapels made of bark and the big thatched churches are decked with bright flowers and green palms. The call drum beats out the invitation to all to come to the meeting.

Children and parents put on their best beads and their gayest clothes and crowd into the churches, singing as they go. Choirs and school choruses fill the air with music. And why do they give thanks? Because over seventy-five years ago the first missionary came to their forests and told them the story of Jesus. It is the coming of the good news to their country that they celebrate.

They call the festival *Evamelunga,* "The Taking Away of the Burden of Sin." And so in their festival of rejoicing they tell one another why they are glad. A schoolboy is thankful that he has been taught to read God's Book. A mother is grateful because she is no longer afraid of witchcraft. And all give thanks to God that they have heard about Jesus.

When the meeting is over, there is feasting and singing and laughter far into the night—for the festival of Thanksgiving is a festival of joy.— *Lois McNeill*

GREETINGS OF AFRICA

In Africa south of the Sahara, greetings are often accompanied by the clapping of cupped hands.

ANGOLA

Kalunga?	Are you well?
Response—*Ku ku*	Yes
A farewell—*Ewa*	Go well

CONGO

In the morning—*Oatso?*	Are you awake?
Response—*O*	Yes
During the day—*Oleko?*	Are you there?
Response—*O*	Yes
A common greeting—*Moyo!*	Life to you!

EGYPT

One greeting is common to all holidays, religious or otherwise, including birthdays:

Kulli sana wi inta tayyib!	The whole year and may you have well-being!

Easter greeting used by older Christians:

Rabbuna qam	Our Lord is risen
Response—*Haqqan qam*	He is risen indeed

NATAL, SOUTH AFRICA

Wer ka mal	Go well
Be duoth ka mal	Stay well

NIGERIA

In the morning—*Kana lafiya?* (*Kana* spoken to a man, *kina* to a woman)	Are you well?
Response—*Lafiya*	Well

Greetings in Kulung and Hausa:
Maraba	Welcome
A welcome—*Yu manan*	Come well
A farewell—*Kya manan*	Go well

Sierra Leone
Tana massi	Good morning
Tana ma talane	Good day
Mbe sohoma	Good-bye
Innu walli	Thank you

Southern Rhodesia
Gi cile	The sun is risen
E, ndi vukile	Yes, I am awake

West Africa—Cameroun
Mbolo	Greetings
W'aso vé?	Where do you come from?
W'ake vé?	Where are you going?
Ye ô ne mvóé?	Are you well?
Ya, me ne mvóé?	Yes, I'm well
Akéva foo	Thanks be
Wulu mvoé	Walk in peace
Me keya	Good-bye (literally, I've gone, or I'm away)

Zulu
Sakubona (singular)	Good morning
Sanibona (plural)	
Uyaphila na? (singular)	How are you?
Niyaphila na? (plural)	

: 3 :

Asia

FOLK FESTIVALS

Burma

THE WATER FESTIVAL

The Water Festival, or New Year's feast, is celebrated by everyone in all parts of Burma. The Burmese year begins in the spring, with the month of Tagoo, and New Year's Day falls between our ninth and twelfth of April, usually on April 11.

On New Year's Eve, everyone sits up and at midnight a cannon goes off to announce the arrival of the new year. All who have guns rush outside and fire them. Then all the people come out of their houses, carrying earthen pots full of water, with fresh green leaves and twigs from a sacred tree on the top. The head of the house recites a prayer, and then the water is poured on the ground. After that a few go back to bed, but most of the people stay up and talk until morning.

As soon as it begins to get light, the people in the house

take jars of clean water to one of the Buddhist monasteries where they present them to the monks. After they return home, the fun begins. All along the road are children and young people with water containers of various kinds—cups, bowls, bamboo goblets, squirt guns—all throwing water at one another and at passers-by. By breakfast time everyone is wet through, but no one minds, for this is the hottest time of the year, and the water feels delightfully cool.

During the day people go around to pay their respects to their friends and business associates, and everywhere the water-throwing goes on. Some people go down to the river, wade in, and splash water on one another until they get tired. No one ever gets angry, and there is much good-humored fun and jollity. The feast lasts for several days and no one wants to be seen with dry clothes as that would show he had no friends and was unpopular.

On the last day a gun is fired at noon and then the feast is over.—*Lucy Wiatt*

THE FEAST OF LIGHTS

The most beautiful festival in Burma is the Feast of Lights, a time of rejoicing for young and old. It occurs in October and in celebrating it, the fronts of the houses are so artistically decorated with lights that one walks as in fairyland. This lighting is usually done with candles, set into transparent paper cornucopias with lumps of clay and fastened on long sticks. The sticks are then put into the ground in such arrangements that the colored cornucopias make pretty patterns of light. The children carry paper toys, such as birds, with lights inside, or they push lighted paper carts or paper automobiles. The toys are made of

very thin paper, either colored or white, so that the light which is set inside shines through.

In the evening children and grown people go around and visit one another and admire the decorations. Sweetmeats made of coconut, *sago*, *suggyi* (a cereal like cream of wheat), nuts, and raisins are served to the visitors.—*Marian Reifsneider* (See also pages 52, 130.)

HARVEST FEAST

In the month of November, when the first harvest is over and the rice has been reaped, the prosperous Burmese farmer usually makes a gift of a certain number of baskets of rice to the monks in the nearest Buddhist monastery and also to his friends and neighbors. This festival is called the *Htamanè-hto*. *Htamanè* is made of sticky rice mixed with sliced coconut, sesame seeds, ginger, and onions, all boiled together. It is very delicious but somewhat indigestible, too. In preparation for the party, the farmer sends boys out with packets of *la-hpet* (pickled tea leaf) to all the young men in the neighborhood, inviting them to come and help him husk his rice for the *htamanè*.

The young men come in the evening, just at dark, bringing their wooden mortars and pestles with them. Before they settle down to work, everyone has some tea and a bit of sociability. Then while the young men are husking the rice, the girls and young women prepare the dishes, lacquer trays, and plantain leaves on which the *htamanè* will be placed when finished, and also get ready the onions, coconut, sesame seeds, and ginger. As they work, they take turns entertaining the party—some with songs, both serious and humorous; and some with stories, especially ghost stories. There is much laughter and chattering, and everyone eats pickled tea leaf, which helps to keep them awake until the *htamanè* is cooked. After a while the children go to bed, but the next morning the boys are allowed to go to the Buddhist monastery with their fathers, carrying the *htamanè* in lacquer boxes and presenting it to the monks.

The girls, meanwhile, have the fun of dressing up in their best, with flowers in their hair, and taking gifts of *htamanè* to all their friends and neighbors.—*Lucy Wiatt*

BIRTHDAY

The Burmese children do not make as much of birthdays as we do. In fact, many of them find it hard to tell you the actual date of their birth. But anyone can tell you the day of the week on which he was born. This is very important to him, because a Burmese child is named according to the day of the week on which he was born. The letters of the alphabet are divided up and assigned to the different days of the week as follows:

Sunday—all the vowels
Monday—k, g, ng
Tuesday—s, z, ny
Wednesday—l, w (from noon to midnight—y)
Thursday—p, b, m
Friday—th, h
Saturday—t, d, n

If you were born on a Thursday, for instance, your name would have to begin with a p, b, or m; for example, Maung Pah (Mr. Frog) or Ma Myint (Miss Tall). If you were born on a Friday, your name might be Ma Hla Thin (Miss Beautiful and Learned) or Maung Than (Mr. Voice).

Many Burmese believe that a man's character is determined by the day of his birth. Thus anyone born on Sunday will probably be stingy; on Monday, jealous; on Tuesday, honest; on Wednesday, cranky; on Thursday, gentle; on Friday, talkative; and on Saturday, quarrelsome.

Every child is expected to have a birth certificate, which is a sort of horoscope drawn up by an astrologer. This is made of a folded strip of

palm leaf and gives the name of the person, and the hour, day, month, and year of his birth, according to the Burmese calendar; also the planet under which he was born, and a number of squares, figures, etc. For all important events in his life he is supposed to consult the astrologer, who, by calculations based on these figures, will determine what are the most suitable and lucky days and hours for him.
—*Lucy Wiatt*

China

NEW YEAR

The New Year celebration, the most important and gayest of all Chinese festivals, takes place on the first day of their first month, falling somewhere between our January 21 and February 19. It is mainly a festival of the home, but indirectly it affects the whole community. For one thing it is the birthday of all Chinese, each one becoming a year older on that day, even though born but twenty-four hours before.

The preparations for the festival begin weeks in advance. The womenfolk clean the house thoroughly and see that needed repairs are made. They purchase or make new clothes and shoes for each member of the family—or as many as can be afforded. They make ready the foods for the festival.

Meanwhile the men are engaged in setting their business affairs in order. Debts are paid and collected. Business books are balanced and closed. Pieces of red paper are placed on the window sills and doors of the home to ward off evil and bring good luck.

On New Year's Eve all shops are closed and people retire within their homes. They dress themselves in their new clothes. Quietly they eat together the last meal of the old year. Everyone stays up until midnight to say farewell to the old year and to greet the new.

Just before midnight the doors of the home are locked and sealed with good luck papers. At midnight the younger members of the family salute their elders in low bows called *kowtows,* at the same time wishing them "New happiness for the New Year!" Then the family goes to bed.

Early in the morning of the next day, the seals on the door are broken. That day the family spends at home, quietly worshiping their ancestors and being very polite and gentle to each other.

On the second festival day the people go into the streets, giving the New Year greeting, "I wish that you may have joy" and receiving the reply, "May joy be with you."

On the third and fourth days the children go about in groups from house to house, singing, in the hope of being given rewards of rice cakes or oranges.

The festival continues for two weeks with music and play-acting in the streets and joy in the homes.

This feast is celebrated in Hong Kong, Hawaii, Taiwan (Formosa), and in North America, wherever a group of Chinese people are living.

THE FEAST OF LANTERNS

On the third day of the celebrations held during the Chinese New Year, which falls between January 21 and February 19, comes the Feast of Lanterns, a day the children particularly enjoy. People vie with one another in getting lanterns of various shapes, colors, and sizes to hang in gardens, on porches, in streets, and in temples.

On the evening of this festival a great parade is held. People come out into the streets carrying lighted lanterns and join the parade, which is led by a huge dragon. The dragon, which is a symbol of goodness and strength, is a great empty shell made of bamboo covered with silk or paper and painted most realistically. Men walk inside the shell of the dragon all along its length, carrying it on their shoulders, with only their feet showing. So the dragon moves along the street, curving like a great snake. It can turn its head from side to side and open and shut its big red mouth, showing fierce teeth inside.

Crowds gather along the street to watch. They shout and set off firecrackers and make a great deal of noise.

DRAGON BOAT FESTIVAL

More than 2400 years ago in China, which was then divided into seven warring countries, there lived a clever prime minister named Ch'u Yüan. He loved his country dearly and was skillful in keeping it out of war. Unfortunately his political enemies were jealous of him and accused him of wrongdoing to the Emperor, who had him exiled to an obscure town.

Ch'u Yüan became very sad and wrote a poem called *"Li Sao,"* which means "Parting Sorrow." This poem told

of his love for his country and his desire to keep it from war. His distress was so great that he drowned himself in the river, on the fifth day of the fifth moon, or month, Chinese calendar.

After his death, many people read his poem and realized that he loved his country deeply. Over the years the people revered his memory. In honor of Ch'u Yüan they hold a great festival on the fifth of the fifth moon. They hang sweet-smelling herbs at the tops of their doors and windows on the anniversary of the day Ch'u Yüan died. Since they believe that his spirit is still in the water of rivers, they provide food for it by throwing rice balls into the rivers.

Rice balls are made of cooked rice and are the size of small oranges. In the middle of the balls are chopped peanuts, brown beans with sugar, fruit, or chopped meat. They are wrapped in bamboo leaves to keep them fresh and clean.

The fishermen along the rivers used to go out in their boats to sacrifice their rice. Gradually the custom of having boat races on the fifth of the fifth moon developed. Special boats are built, and on their fronts are carved dragons. The festival is now usually called the Dragon Boat Festival. The Chinese people who left the mainland and moved to Taiwan (Formosa) still celebrate this festival.

Children enjoy the day because their parents take them to see the dragon boat races, give them rice balls to eat, and teach them to throw rice balls into the river.

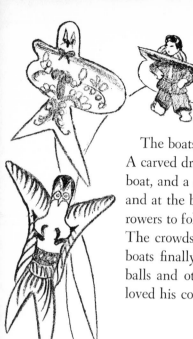

The boats used in the races are long and narrow and shallow in depth. A carved dragon's head, painted and gilded, is placed on the bow of the boat, and a colorful tail at the stern. In each boat there are many rowers and at the back are two men who beat out on gongs the rhythm for the rowers to follow. The boats are lined up and swoop off at a given signal. The crowds on the bank shout and yell to cheer them on. One of the boats finally wins, and everyone goes home delighted to feast on rice balls and other good food. And the name of Ch'u Yüan, a man who loved his country, is thus revered.—*Eleanor Anderson*

KITE FLYING

The Kite Flying Festival is for both men and boys. It comes on the ninth day of the ninth moon, or month, by the Chinese calendar. A week or so ahead of the festival, stores display kites of all kinds and sizes. Some boys make their own kites, using bamboo sticks for the lightweight frames. Many sizes and shapes of paper are spread across the various frames. This handmade paper is thin, yet very tough.

On the morning of the festival day, strange and beautiful kites may be seen moving down the narrow streets of the city. Eager boys carry them to the broad city wall or out to the hills and open places along the river. Soon the sky is alive and gay with kites of all sizes, resembling huge bats, flowers, butterflies, scorpions, fish, and dragons.

On some dragon kites the eyes are cleverly made to revolve in the breeze, and the very long tails wave in the wind. The boys play tricks with the flying kites. One boy will try to cross another's kite string with his own. Then he works his own string back and forth to cut the other's kite string. This is a signal that his kite has won over the other's.

Thousands of people spend the day watching the antics of the kites and thoroughly enjoy the sport. Suddenly someone will say, "Oh, there is Han Shin!" And all those who hear will try to spot the special kite that is shaped like a fat little man. For the Chinese people believe that long, long ago (200 B.C.), the first kite to appear in China skies was flown by Han Shin, a clever dwarf, who is supposed to have used this first kite in a unique way to win a battle for his country. They remember him to this day by flying kites shaped to look like him.—*Beulah E. Bassett*

India

MAKRA SANKRANT

This is a seasonal festival which comes at the time of the winter solstice (the point at which the sun is farthest from the equator) in January. It is observed all over India for three days, especially by Hindu women and children, and its name tends to vary somewhat according to the region in which the festival is celebrated.

Makra Sankrant (sometimes *Makara Sankranti*), which celebrates the coming of longer days, is a day for family reunions; for giving of alms to the poor and to the priests; and for bathing in rivers.

The special sweets and cakes made for the festival always contain *til* and *ghur* (sesame seed and brown sugar). On the first day of *Sankrant* everyone gets up early and has a bath, then puts on his best clothes. Women fill small clay pots with gram seeds, berries, and other similar foods. Turmeric and red powder are rubbed on the outside of the jars. The decorated pots are given away to neighbor women.

Special food is prepared for the festival, particularly a spiral-shaped candy, similar to a *jelabi*. A whole wheat bread with brown sugar in the middle is another delicacy; also a coarse brown bread with sesame seed on top. The children like this festival because they get so much sweet food. *Til* (sesame) seeds, in tiny sugar pellets, are given to friends with the greeting, "Eat this sweet sesame and speak sweetly to me," intended to end all quarreling throughout the year. Small silk bags of the sweet are often sent to friends.—*Virginia McKenzie Parker*

THE FESTIVAL OF LIGHTS

Divali or *Dipavali,* the Hindu New Year, falls in October or November and is celebrated throughout India. It comes at the end of the monsoon rains, when the weather is pleasant and mild, and lasts from three to five days. It is a time of rejoicing and giving gifts.

Daughters return home to visit. Houses are freshly cleaned; walls whitewashed and decorated with designs drawn in white rice flour water, and then filled in with color. Business account books are closed and new ones opened ceremoniously. New clothes are worn. Friends are entertained.

Early in the morning of the first day of the festival all the members of the family rise early and take a perfumed bath and are anointed with oil and perfume by the mother. They then put on new clothes and enjoy a breakfast of fourteen different kinds of food, especially prepared for the occasion.

At dusk on the first three festival days, houses and shops are decorated with lights. Traditionally, small saucers of oil with tiny cotton wicks are placed so that they outline roofs, doors, and windows. Some people use instead strings of electric lights. Fireworks are set off.

Children share in all this activity, enjoying the foods and sweets. Special *puries* (thin fried wheat cakes), *karunjies* (coconut, sugar, and spice filled pastries), and *laddus* (milk, sugar, and pulse, boiled to make candy) are eaten. In Maharashtra, boys build elaborate model forts and castles of mud, decorating them with tiny trees, animals, and their favorite warriors. These are displayed to friends who call, and there is a keen sense of competition among the young teen-agers.

People who live along the rivers fasten lighted lamps to little rafts of bamboo or plantain stalks, and set them afloat on the water. The children shout with joy and clap their hands at the pretty sight of hundreds of twinkling lights floating down the river.

In South India the children wear wreaths of flowers around their heads, bracelets on their arms, and bells around their ankles.—*Virginia McKenzie Parker*

BROTHER AND SISTER DAY

The fifth day of *Divali* is *Bhau-Beez* (Brother's Day or Brother and Sister Day). At this time, the brother and sister relationship is celebrated and gifts are exchanged. While the sister lives at home, she prepares warm water for her brother's morning bath and scented oil for his massage. She bathes him, if he is small. When she is married, and returns to her old home, she supplies the food for her brother on that day. She arranges a special low stool, drawing decorative designs on the floor around it, and in the evening the brother is seated there, facing east. She puts on his forehead the *tilak* (vertical line) of *kumkum* (red powder). She then performs the *ovalni*, waving two small lamps on a brass tray, ceremoniously, and prays for him. She also throws a few grains of rice on his head wishing him long and safe life. This is called the *ackshate*. Her usual gift to him is food, since she does not earn money.

In return, the brother puts a gift for his sister on the tray—jewelry, a *sari,* a piece of cloth for a blouse, or money. A girl with many brothers is considered fortunate. Later in the day the girl compares gifts with those of her friends. When they are adults, the brother may go to his sister's home for the ceremony. Should he be away, he will send a gift, perhaps of money. When a mother has sons only, she invites a cousin or the daughter of a friend to be their "sister." This relationship may last through life. If a girl has no brother, or he is far away, she may do *ovalni* and *ackshate* to the moon and "is sad." But in general the festival is one of joy.—*Virginia McKenzie Parker*

India—Kerala

ONAM

The Hindu harvest festival known as *Onam* comes in September and is celebrated by all the people, regardless of caste or creed. Even the poorest will try to have some new garment for this occasion and some food for a feast. The peasants gladly welcome the sunny month of harvest after the rainy monsoon season. The festival lasts for four days. For *Onam* the landlords distribute rice and cloth to their tenants, who in return make token presents from the produce of the fields. Everyone, young and old, takes part in the games, music, and dancing. There is a special day given over to the children and they receive presents of new cloth from the shops from their parents and relatives. Children have special enjoyment at this time with *oonjals* or swings. A child sits on the swing seat while another pushes him forward with an *oonjal* song.

At the feast, vegetarian food is served, and it is eaten from plantain leaves. In Hindu homes beautiful floral designs prepared by the women are often set up in the courtyards.—*Gordon A. Schieck*

India—North

BASWANT

In North India and in Pakistan, the spring festival is called *Baswant* or *Baswanta,* which in Sanskrit means yellow, the sacred color in India and a symbol of spring. During this festival, everyone wears yellow in some part of his clothing.

The family fast until noon and place an offering of food and white flowers before the image of the goddess of learning, Saraswati. They then go to an open field for a picnic lunch together and to enjoy the out of doors.

This is the season for kite flying and the boys and the fathers of the families like to fly their gay, flat, tailless kites, made of colored tissue paper and bamboo. As in many Asian countries the first hundred feet of the kite's string is often covered with a glue holding ground glass so that it can cut the string of another kite whose string it crosses. Fights between flying kites become very exciting. Boys chase after the freed kites, hoping to capture one as it falls to the ground.—*Virginia McKenzie Parker*

THE THREAD CEREMONY

In North India, the Hindu festival of *Raksha Bandham,* the Thread Ceremony, comes after the rains in late July or early August. On this day a sister gives or sends a *raki,* a bracelet of colored threads, to her brother. By this she signifies that she needs his protection. If a girl has no brother, the family arranges for a cousin or a very close family friend to take the part of the brother.

In the thread-tying ceremony, the sister touches her brother's forehead with red powder in blessing. She then ties the bracelet around her brother's wrist, and presents him with food she has prepared herself. In return the brother gives her money and other gifts. After the ceremony, a party is held for the special guests who have been invited for the occasion.

The bracelet is like an amulet and it is supposed to protect the brother from harm during the coming year. By wearing it he pledges himself to protect his sister in time of need.

India—South

PONGAL

Pongal is the *Sankrant* festival of South India, celebrated on January 11, 12 or 13. It is a time of thanksgiving for rain and sunshine that made the harvest and of prayer for good crops in the future. Women and children observe it particularly. On the first morning the people are awakened by the sound of music made by little tap drums held in one hand and tapped with the fingers of the other. On rising, the women and children rub *til* (sesame) oil on their bodies and then bathe. The family gathers in the courtyard of the house where a small stove has been set up and a new pot placed on it. Into the pot goes some of the recently harvested rice, some peas, beans and lentils, sugar, and milk. The members of the family, of all ages, join hands and move around

the pot in time to the tapping of the drums. When the pot boils, they shout gaily *"pongal"* (it boils) because the quick boiling of the pot means a prosperous year. The children look forward to eating some of the delicacy just prepared.—*Virginia McKenzie Parker*

DOLL FESTIVAL

A South Indian festival, chiefly for women and girls, is *Navaratri*, or Doll Festival. It begins with the Hindu month Ashwin and usually falls in our October. It lasts for nine days, which are filled with entertainment.

In a special place in each house there is placed a copper or silver dish, which is filled with rice and covered with coconut and mango leaves to represent the Divine Mother, the Hindu goddess Durga. Toys and dolls are placed in rows around the walls of the room, representing gods, men, and animals. Festoons of colored paper and flowers are used to decorate the room.

This is a time when women and girls, wearing their best clothes, visit in one another's homes. Music and dancing are part of the entertainment in each home, the guests as well as the hostess taking part. Girls sing to the goddess as they hold hands and move in a slow circular dance. The hostess gives gifts of coconuts, cakes, and *pan supari* (betel nut) to her guests as they leave.—*Virginia McKenzie Parker*

Indonesia

THE FEAST OF RICE

In this new nation of Indonesia, with the exception of Independence Day, the festivals celebrated are mainly tribal ones.

In late July, in the fertile valleys of central Sulawesi (Celebes) where the Toradja tribes live, comes *Pesta Padi,* the Feast of Rice. At that time the heavy yellow rice stalks have been cut and laid out on the mats in fat, short bundles. Everyone, both young and old, has helped with the harvest, and all celebrate the three day feast together. *Pesta Padi* is an ancient feast, but because the Toradja tribes became Christian long ago, they give thanks to God during the festival, even though they continue to use its ancient forms.

As soon as the sun is low enough for comfort, the people gather in a big open space at the edge of the village. The boys, wearing bright new sarongs, come together for the exciting game of *sepa-kaki,* foot kicking. The village chief divides them into two rival teams of equal numbers. After shouting challenges to one another, boys of the opposing teams line up against each other. Their sarongs are girded closely about their waists and they hold hands tightly. The boys of each team try to down their opponents one by one, by kicking and pushing them with their feet. When all the members of one team are downed, new challengers line up. The game is rough, but the boys would not think of missing the fun.

After the *sepa-kaki* contest, comes the feast—*mami-mami-mia,* they call it. Sections of young bamboo, filled with new rice and coconut milk, chicken and fish, are cooked on the glowing charcoals of the fire. Then the deliciously cooked food is served on squares of green banana leaves and eaten with the fingers.

Everyone sits around the fire after the feast. Then one of the men begins to strum softly on a stringed instrument called a *gandang* and starts an ancient song of happiness about the rice harvest. Others join in the song and clap to the music. Soon a great circle is formed, and people dance and sing around the fire, the children joining them. festival goes on in this way for three days.—*Mrs. F. W. Brandauer*

Iran

NEW YEAR

In Iran, New Year's Day, *No-ruz,* is March 21, the first day of spring. The observance is a very old one, dating back to old Persia and pre-Islamic times. This is an appropriate time to celebrate the beginning of a new year, for in many places almond trees are in blossom and weeping willows are showing fresh green leaves.

Preparations for this important festival begin weeks in advance. The mother of the family puts a piece of cloth in an earthen bowl or on a plate, wets it, and sprinkles wheat or lentil seeds on it. By keeping it moist until the time of the feast, it becomes a lovely dish of growing green.

Everyone has new clothes for *No-ruz,* and the week before the festival the big housecleaning of the year (the house-shaking, as it is called) takes place. A day or two before *No-ruz* the whole family goes to the public bath.

The last night of the old year, each family places small piles of desert thorn, several yards apart, in their own yard or out in the street. At dusk

the piles are lighted, and everyone, young and old, runs pell-mell down the line laughing and shouting as they jump over each little bonfire. As they run, they call out to the fire, "My paleness (ill health) go to you; your redness (good health) come to me."

The new year begins just as the sun crosses the equator. The time is carefully estimated in advance, and notice is given. In small villages a gun is often fired. In large cities a cannon sometimes booms out the news. Whenever the notice comes, the whole family, dressed in their new clothing, must be gathered around a table or a cloth spread on the floor. On the cloth are placed the bowls of growing cereal and a tray with *haft seen* (meaning seven S's), seven articles of food the names of which begin with the Persian letter S, such as *sabzi* (herbs), *seerke* (vinegar), and so on. For each member of the family there is a lighted candle, and if possible, a goldfish in a glass bowl. It is believed that at the moment the year changes, the fish turns over in the water!

When the gun or cannon goes off, each person says, "May your new year be blessed!" The first meal of the new year will include *kababs* (meat and vegetables on a skewer) if the family can afford lamb, and there must be rice cooked in a special way with fresh herbs, and smoked fish. Sometimes there are toys for the children, but the most important thing is the new clothes.

For the twelve days of the feast everybody goes to visit his friends. On the first day, if possible, the parents take the children to see their grandparents. The children kneel on the floor beside their grandmother and kiss her hand. The grandmother kisses them on both cheeks and gives each of them some silver coins or perhaps a gold piece. Wherever they

go, there are many delicious tiny cakes and many kinds of candy. Everyone, even the children, drinks many glasses of very sweet tea. Every child goes home with his pockets full of *ajeel* (roasted dried peas, dried mulberries, raisins, pistachio nuts, roasted squash and watermelon seeds).

On the last day of the celebration the whole family must go out of the house and, if possible, outside of the town or city. They take their lunch and a samovar for making tea, and have an all-day picnic beside some irrigation stream. On this day the bowls of green wheat are thrown out into the running stream or into the street, a sign that all illness, bad luck, ill-feeling, and family quarrels are cast away. And so, for the children of Iran, the most wonderful time of the whole year ends.— *Mrs. Arthur C. Boyce*

Iraq

BREAKING OF THE FAST

The Breaking of the Fast, *Eed-al-Fittir,* is celebrated by Muslims everywhere, including Syria, Jordan, Iraq, and Morocco. It marks the end of the fifth lunar month, called Ramadan, the time of fasting that is followed by all true Muslims, who do not eat or drink between sunrise and sundown for each day of that month. During Ramadan all eating by the faithful Muslim is done before sunrise or after sunset.

Then comes *Eed-al-Fittir,* a time of joy and feasting. The beginning of the festival may be announced by the booming of cannon or the beating of drums. For three days everyone stops work and celebrates.

A great deal of attention is paid to the children. For days before, mothers shop for or sew new clothes, so that the boys may have bright new sateen blouses and the girls gay silk dresses. All the young people go to the village or town square where they find swings, merry-go-rounds, and perhaps a ferris wheel. There may also be puppet shows.

Hot roasted chestnuts, salted peanuts, and watermelon seeds are on sale.

When the sun has set, everyone goes home to eat the special foods that have been prepared. Particular favorites are a kind of wheat-and-meat ball, fried in deep fat, called *kibbie,* and a sweet made of many layers of pastry, soaked in honey, called *baklava.* Family gatherings take place on the following evenings, and the children receive gifts from their parents and relatives. On the third day the mother finds time to go visiting, too. The festival is a time of rejoicing for the whole family.
—*Mrs. Alford Carleton*

Israel

YOM KIPPUR

Yom Kippur, the Day of Atonement, is the most solemn day of the Jewish year. It comes at the end of summer, and it is of very ancient origin.

Yom Kippur brings to a close the Ten Days of Penitence that begin with Rosh Hashanah, the First of the Year. These are very holy days—ten days of grace during which a person passes judgment on his own life and has the chance to change it for the better, through prayer, penitence, and charity.

Yom Kippur is a solemn day of fasting for the adults. No work is done and the day is a serious one. Dressed in white, the families go to the synagogue. At a solemn service they confess their sins and pray for forgiveness. As the first star of evening appears in the sky, a horn is blown in the synagogue and the people hurry home to break their fast. They give greetings to friends and relatives saying, "May your fate be sealed for a good year!"

In Jewish homes a feast is served and everyone is happy. The tables are loaded with many tasty dishes, among them apples dipped in honey, served to express the hope that the new year will be sweet and happy.

The festivals of Succoth and Hanukkah (see pages 125 and 126) are also observed in Israel.

Japan

NEW YEAR

In Japan on the first day of the first month, January 1, the greatest holiday of all is celebrated. For one thing, everybody has a birthday on that day, even month-old babies. On the day you are born you are already one year old; you stay one until the New Year, when you are two.

If possible, everyone goes home to celebrate the New Year. It is a very busy time in the home. Houses are scrubbed clean; entrances are decorated with pine boughs, bamboo, and other symbols of long life and happiness. All bills must be paid by midnight before the great day, so people scurry about settling accounts.

If the family can afford it, everyone must have something new to wear for the occasion. If the children's battledore and shuttlecock got broken last year, a new set must be had for this day. Quantities of rice must be steamed and pounded to pulp and then molded into big round cakes, called *omochi*. Children stand in the streets, watching the special men who come to the house to make the cakes and who wear blue towels around their heads. With rhythmic shouts they pound the rice to make the New Year cakes, which are served during the following days.

In every home, New Year's breakfast is a ceremonial meal when *ozoni*, a soup, and special dishes are served. Doors stand open, revealing trays of colored *omochi*, often piled before a beautiful screen. Everyone wears his best clothes. Children in gay kimonos and new shoes play in the streets with balls or battledores, much decorated, and brightly colored feather-tipped shuttlecocks. When friends meet, they bow and congratulate each other. For three days, stores are closed while people visit or feast their guests, and enjoy the holiday.—*Mrs. Robert Spencer*

GIRLS' FESTIVAL

Doll Day is a festival for little Japanese girls. It always falls on the third day of the third month, March 3, the month of cherry blossoms, and so the lovely decorations for this festival are cherry blossoms. The festival lasts three days and it is observed as it was centuries ago.

Nearly every girl in Japan owns a doll festival set. In the principal room of the house a set of five steps is placed and covered with a red cloth. The dolls are arranged on the steps, with their furniture and belongings. On the highest step are two dolls in elaborate dress who represent the Emperor and Empress. Behind them is placed a folding screen.

On the second step stand two square pots of unpainted white wood, holding artificial trees—a cherry on the right, an orange on the left. On the third step are the ladies-in-waiting, who are supposed to serve their master and mistress on the step above. On the fourth step are five musicians; and on the fifth various household articles.

The little girl cares for all the articles during the three days of the feast. Dressed in a formal kimono, she entertains friends, serves her visitors with tea and little cakes, beautifully made and displayed in tiers.

During this season Japanese stores sell all sorts of tiny

articles, for use during the festival. After the festival, the
dolls and the furniture are carefully put away in a chest,
to be kept there until the next year. Some of the festival
dolls are very old. A girl may have in her set dolls that be-
longed to her grandmother and her mother.—*Ursula Moran*

BOYS' FESTIVAL

The boys of Japan have a special day of their own,
celebrated on the fifth day of the fifth month. On that day,
May 5, tall bamboo poles appear in the front of the houses
where boys live. The poles may be nailed on the front of
the house or placed upright in front of it. Fastened on a
strong cord to the top of the pole are great colored banners
made of cloth or paper, one banner for each boy in the
household. Each banner is in the shape of a big fish and
it is painted in bright colors to look like a fish. The fish
has an open mouth, and as it flutters from the pole, the
wind blows into the mouth, filling the banner so that it
floats in the air as a fish would in the stream. The fish are
supposed to represent carp, a strong fish, brave enough to
leap a waterfall. A Japanese boy is supposed to grow strong
and brave like the carp. Often the boy is given a bath in
water that has iris leaves or petals in it. These are supposed
to give him strength.

FESTIVAL OF THE DEAD

On August 13, the *O Bon Matsuri,* Festival of the Dead, is held in Buddhist homes. At this time, the spirits of the family's ancestors are supposed to return for a visit.

For days in advance there is a great cleaning of the home. Special foods are prepared and lanterns are hung in the cemeteries. A miniature boat is built for the return voyage of the spirits.

On August 13, just at dusk, parents and children light a welcoming fire of small sticks in front of each house. Doors stand wide open, candles are burning high on the god-shelf, before the ancestral tablets. Places are set at low tables for the spirit guests. Each family kneels on their mats to enjoy the feast, as though the spirit relatives were indeed present.

For three days the spirits are entertained. Then fires are lit to speed the spirits on their way, and at midnight the family goes to the beach or riverbank carrying their small boat, loaded with food, and aglow with tiny candles. There a man or boy of the family pushes the boat into the water. Imagine the sight of scores of lighted boats drifting off on the water, watched by throngs of quiet, reverent people.—*Mrs. Robert Spencer*

MOON VIEWING

The October moon is supposed to be the brightest full moon of the year, and October the most perfect month as far as weather is concerned. So on the night of full moon, hundreds of people walk out into the country, or up a mountain, or to the seashore, or anywhere where they can get a clear view for the "Moon Viewing."

On this occasion, everyone sings or whistles or plays the harmonica, making music as he goes. When they arrive at their favorite moon viewing place, they stand and drink in the beauty before them, and the adults often write poems about it. As the family walk home, they gather some of the wild grasses by the roadside to make flower arrangements, to place in the most honored spot in the home. There are seven kinds of grasses called the Seven Grasses of Autumn which they can gather, and they always try to have them all.—*Ursula Moran*

Korea

NEW YEAR

In Korea the children look forward eagerly to New Year's Day. It comes either the last of January or the first of February.

Every child, except the very poorest ones, has a new bright-colored suit or dress for this day, and there is certain to be a coin bag fastened to his belt with cords.

Early that morning the children bow to all of the older members of their family, going first to the eldest. They bow gracefully and so low that their heads almost touch the floor. After he rises, each child is given a coin by every older person, to put into his bag.

Then the children start out gaily to visit the houses of their relatives and friends. They politely bow to each of the older persons, and are given coins for their bags. They are also invited to eat some of the holiday food, such as honey cakes and barley candy, and needless to say they always accept. They come home and show what they have gathered in their bags.

The rest of the day is spent playing, the girls practicing juggling and jumping on a kind of seesaw and the boys flying kites. The boys have exciting contests to see which

one can make his kite fly the highest or stay up **the** longest.
—*Mrs. Virginia Fairfax*

SWING DAY

Swing Day, which comes in the fifth moon, is a jolly time for Korean children. They go with their families to beautiful groves of trees to spend the day.

The girls go with the women to a grove where swings hang from the largest trees. When the girls in their bright-colored dresses are swinging high among the green branches, they look like flying birds with brilliant feathers. The children's favorite food on that day is *gegime* (hot cakes), sold by women who bake them over hot coals in a brazier.

The boys go with the men to another grove and have wrestling matches. They have practiced wrestling for weeks in advance. Proud, indeed, are the boys who win prizes for their skill.—*Mrs. Virginia Fairfax*

Pakistan

FEAST OF THE GIFT

'Id ul Fitr, the Feast of the Gift, is the most important Muslim festival and is the most enjoyed by the children. It follows Ramadan, the month of fasting decreed by the prophet Muhammad, during which the faithful do not eat or drink in the hours of daylight. Children are usually not expected to keep the fast.

After a breakfast of *semia,* a cereal cooked in milk with plenty of sugar, the men and boys go to the mosque for prayers, while the women and girls perform their prayers at home.

The rest of the day is spent in receiving guests, going to visit relatives and friends, playing games, enjoying 'Id gifts. Sometimes these are toys, but usually they take the form of money gifts, put into new little bags. The children look forward with great glee to spending their money exactly as they wish.

The people always share their feast with the poor and give clothes to them also. They feel that the day should be one of blessing, not only during the feast, but throughout the whole year.—*Mrs. J. M. Benade*

Syria

HARVEST FEAST

In Syria it is the custom to boil part of the wheat before it is stored. In some villages the boiling is done in a large community pot, a brass cauldron that stands in the middle of the village, and a feast is held at that time. The pot may be used by all the people and a fire is kept burning under it continuously during the harvest season. One householder after another takes his turn boiling his wheat.

The girls of the village do most of the work of boiling the wheat. Some of them bring water from the village well, carrying it in jars on their heads. Some bring grain from their own store of wheat. If the ceremony is at night, a man with a lighted lantern goes with them. Soon the wheat is bubbling in the cauldron and the helpers dance around the fire, singing and playing games until the wheat is ready. Then the householder serves them bowls of newly cooked wheat, made more tasty by the addition of nuts and sweets. After the feast the girls carry the boiled wheat to the householder's home, where it is spread out to dry on the roof before being stored.

Thailand

NEW YEAR

The happiest days of the year for Thai boys and girls are the five days at *Pee Mai,* or New Year, which come in April. For days the fathers and older boys of the village work at making a great image, perhaps a pagoda, on a bamboo frame covered with multicolored tissue paper. This is placed on runners and a long rope is attached to it.

On the day of the full moon the villagers gather around the pagoda, dressed in their brightest clothes. Some of the men and boys take hold of the rope and start to drag the pagoda to the Buddhist temple.

In front, the elders set the pace with a stately dance. Then comes a host of boys, shouldering a long drum made of a hollow log with skin stretched over the ends. Boys beat the drum with their fingers and others strike gongs as they move along. The gay pagoda, decorated with paper flags, follows with an enormous *bawk fai,* "it speaks fire," inside. Last come the women, bearing silver bowls filled with offerings of rice, cigarettes, cakes, and flowers. The children, of course, are running everywhere.

When the procession arrives at the temple, there are other processions coming with their images—green elephants, red dragons with gold spots, blue buffaloes, huge men. The people go into the temple and bow to the image of Buddha, which has been draped in a new yellow robe for the hot season. The women douse the image with water, as a symbol of purification. They light tapers and place them on the altar, together with their offerings. Then all go outside for a feast of rice, curry, and fruit.

In the afternoon the villagers go into the rice fields and shoot the *bawk fais*. These are made of small pieces of bamboo, bound around a large stick twenty-five feet long, which is filled with gunpowder. When shot into the air, it makes a whistling flutelike sound. On the second day comes the sand festival, when mounds of sand, decorated with paper flags, are placed over the ashes of dead monks.

The ceremony ends with "water throwing" (see *Songkran* below), when people go about carrying silver bowls of scented water. When they greet friends, they throw the scented water at them. Soon everyone is soaked and having a happy time.—*Lucy Starling*

SONGKRAN

Songkran, the Thai Water Festival, is celebrated in the spring, in the middle of April, at the close of the Buddhist New Year festival. It marks the end of the long dry weather and the beginning of the monsoon rains. The festival is associated with water and water throwing.

At the time of this festival, the statues and images of Buddha and of venerable priests are bathed ceremonially and the temple grounds are cleaned and sprinkled with sand from the river. (See previous festival.)

But the fun-loving Thai people enjoy themselves by throwing water at each other for the days of the festival. The people walk up and down the streets, pouring water on all they meet, and getting water poured on them. Some may stand in front of their homes armed with a hose or a water pistol. It's fun if you like to get wet!—*Dr. Harold Hanson*

Turkey

CANDY HOLIDAY

The Candy Holiday, or *Seker Bayrami,* comes at the end of the fast of Ramadan. The time of the holiday moves forward ten days each year, so that sometimes it comes in the summer and sometimes in the spring or fall or winter.

During the month of Ramadan, people who are Muslims refrain from eating, drinking, or smoking all day long. They eat only during the darkness, at night, and in the early morning. Not everyone keeps the fast, but in most families there will be two or three people who do. Sometimes the children are allowed to fast one or two days.

Great preparations are made for the three days of festivities that will follow the end of Ramadan. The father will make a special gift to the poor. He may give money to widows or orphans or a new outfit of clothes to a poor child.

As the great day dawns, everyone dresses in new clothes. Father goes to the mosque in the early morning for "Holiday Prayers." When he returns, his wife kisses his hand and he kisses her on each cheek. Each child greets first his father and then his mother and other grownups with one of the most gracious of gestures—bowing slightly and kissing the hand of each and touching it to his forehead. The grownups give the children pretty handkerchiefs, usually with money wrapped in them. Candy is passed around on a silver or glass plate.

All the family that lives near enough to come has dinner together at the home of the eldest member. In the afternoon, the calling begins. The younger members call on their elder relatives and friends and wish them well, saying, "May your holiday be blessed," and, "We congratulate you on your holiday." Candy is served to all callers, and sometimes small cakes and fruit and small cups of sweetened coffee as well.

Instead of making calls, the children often go to small amusement parks where merry-go-rounds, swings, and puppet shows have been set up.

In the evening, *baklava,* a small flaky pastry, is served. For three days the fun goes on, and then the family settles back into its daily routine, with only the memory of another joyful Candy Holiday.— *Dorothy Blatter*

Vietnam

NEW YEAR

A gay holiday atmosphere prevails in Vietnam as young and old alike prepare for *Tet,* the New Year, which usually falls in February. It is a season for feasting, wearing new clothes, painting shops and houses, and for friendly exchange of gifts.

In many courtyards, a long bamboo pole is set up, decorated with leaves, feathers, tiny bells, little fishes, gold and silver papers, branches of cactus, and a lantern to be lighted at night. On the ground beside the pole is made a whitewash drawing of a bow with its arrow pointing southward, to defend the house against evil spirits. The air is full of the smell of good food being cooked for the feast the next day.

At midnight, on New Year's Eve, each family head offers thanks for the benefits received during the old year and welcomes the new year. After these ceremonies, the people go to the temples to worship.

Dressed in their best clothes the family begins the new year together. Into each home is brought a leafy branch covered with fruit and flowers as a symbol of a happy and prosperous year to come. The family pay respects to their ancestors and then parents and children exchange good wishes for happiness, wealth, and long life.—From *Sunshine,* Church of the Nazarene.

CHRISTIAN FESTIVALS

Burma

CHRISTMAS

The custom of using lights for the celebration of festivals is carried over into the Christian festival of Christmas in some parts of Burma (see Feast of Lights, page 43). Paper stars, lighted inside with candles, are hung on the fronts of the houses. Around the porches or on the walls or fences are tied four-cornered paper cups, containing lighted candles. Or tiny pottery saucers of oil, each with a bit of twisted cloth for a wick, are used. A neat row of these fluttering flames along a wall looks very pretty. The family will have some new clothes—perhaps a silk shirt for the father and new velvet slippers for the daughter.

People who do not know that Christmas is the birthday of Jesus may ask, "Why do you put up lights at this time?"

This question gives members of the Christian family a chance to tell the Christmas story.—*Marian Reifsneider*

India

CHRISTMAS LIGHTS

In parts of India some ceremonies commonly used in the *Divali* festival (see page 52) have been transferred by Christians to the Christmas festivities. This is particularly true in the use of lights for the decoration of the home and its courtyard. At Christmas time, rows of little clay lamps are set along the edge of the roof and the wall of the court-yard. The children of the family are often allowed to fill the lamps with oil and to put a little piece of cotton into the oil to serve as a wick. As darkness falls, the lamps are put in place and lighted, and the whole home glows. Christians often live on the same street of a village, and the row of lighted houses makes a pretty sight.

The newly whitewashed walls of the house are often decorated with stars or other Christian symbols, or with pictures of the Wise Men or the shepherds. The women of the family paint the pictures on the walls, using colored dyes bought in the market.

India—Bengal

BIG DAY

In all the languages of India, Christmas is called Big Day. In Bengal, the church program and the tree on Christmas afternoon are the main interest for Christians.

Every night for weeks the boys and young men gather to practice their songs, with orchestra, for the Christmas pro-gram. The women are busy at home because the house must be cleaned and washed over with fresh clay or whitewash and decorated with leaves, bright-colored paper, and marigolds, to make it look gay to every passer-by. The girls make marigold garlands and colored paper chains for the church.

On Christmas Eve, the boys and young men decorate the church, spending all night at it. By dawn it is gay with wreaths, date palm branches, marigold garlands, and colored paper chains, strung from opposite corners of the building, and the Christmas tree has been set up outside. Then the young men start off to do their Christmas caroling from house to house.

At home, the children dance with joy on Christmas Day, as they eat coconut-filled rice cakes, dates, oranges, raisins, and fruit cake. At noon there is a special rice dinner with meat curry. The children often carry plates of cakes and fruits to the homes of friends.

At two o'clock on Christmas afternoon, the church bell rings, and it is time to put on new clothes that Father has bought for the family. They are all going with Father to the church, which is full to overflowing. The out-of-town guests occupy the places of honor in front.

Printed programs on gay, red paper announce addresses by the pastor and two leading men, and songs by the young men and boys, who sit down in front with all the other boys and girls who can crowd on the mat with them.

The climax comes when all gather around the tree outside. The poor people wait expectantly, knowing there are clothes for them on the tree. The children receive gifts the Sunday school provides—simple but a surprise—in a happy ending to the Big Day.—*Ruth Daniels*

NEW YEAR

For Christian young men and boys in Bengal, New Year's Eve means serenading. After the midnight church service, they announce the New Year with giant firecrackers.

The young men drink cups of hot tea and start off. Some dress to look ridiculous, some wear masks. The leader plays a small organ hung around his neck, and hired Hindu players have huge hornlike instruments. A special kind of antiphonal singing is used and all the songs are religious. Throughout the singing, the young men dance around the leader, moving faster and faster as they sing faster and louder to a breathless climax.

By morning, they are all tired, shivering, and hoarse, but not even the youngest would miss the New Year's church service at nine o'clock. The thank offering is the distinctive feature of this service. Everyone attends and everyone takes his individual gift. This is not collected by the ushers, but at the close of the service all those present, from old and feeble to shy daughters-in-law and little children, carry their gifts to the front in one great joyous procession.

There is still more fun on this day, for the annual Love Feast comes at night when those same young men of last night serve a rice feast to all on the church grounds.—*Ruth Daniels*

India—Kerala

CHRISTMAS

There are large numbers of Christians in Kerala belonging to the Orthodox Syrian Church of Antioch, and the Egyptian Coptic, Armenian, and Abyssinian Churches. Their observances of Christmas and Easter are very elaborate and differ from that of other Christians. For Syrian Christians, Christmas and Easter celebrations mark the end of their two Lenten seasons and are accompanied with pomp and show.

On Christmas Eve, large crowds of people gather in the churches, when the ringing of the bells heralds the coming of Christmas. Drums and pipes are played in relays, and children set off firecrackers to add to the occasion. The churches are fully decorated at this time.

After vespers the congregations disperse for the night, but few of the people go to sleep, as preparations for Christmas Day are begun. At 3 A.M., again heralded by the pealing of bells and display of fireworks, the people congregate and go in procession around the churches. They carry wooden, silver, and gold crosses on pedestals, lighted candles, decorated umbrellas, flags, and torches. The priests, wearing ceremonial vestments and chanting Syriac hymns, accompany the procession. A decorated canopy supported by poles, under which the priests and deacons walk with reverence, is carried by devotees.

The procession returns to the church and the people take part in the Christmas service, which ends at daybreak.

Syrian Lent is a season of partial fasting when people avoid meat, fish, and milk products. On Christmas morning they are eager to taste the good food that has been denied them. They hurry home to prepare hot beef curry, to be eaten with bread made from rice flour and coconut paste. These items form the important part of the Christmas breakfast, after which the children play and the grownups take a much needed rest. In the afternoon, homes of relatives are visited.

The church school sponsors carol singing during the week preceding Christmas. Western carols mingle with Syrian tunes. The young people and their leaders go in lighted processions to the homes of those associated with the work of the church school. They carry lighted candles, fixed inside lanterns made of tissue paper and supported by small poles above the heads of those in the procession.—*Gordon A. Schieck*

EASTER

The night before Easter the people are called to the churches for ceremonies that last until daybreak. A symbolic resurrection is enacted by the priest, using a wooden cross that has been left covered on the altar to show that Jesus had been crucified and buried. Then there is joyful singing accompanied by instrumental music and ringing of bells as the priest announces the good news that the Lord is risen. He lifts the cross out and takes it in procession thrice around the church building. The service ends with the celebration of the Mass and the kissing of the cross by members of the congregation. The black curtain that was hung in front of the altar on Good Friday is replaced by the usual multicolored curtain with variegated designs to indicate the end of the Easter Lenten season. With the close of this joyous celebration of the Resurrection of Christ the people then go back to their homes for feasting and rejoicing.—*Gordon A. Schieck*

India—South Central

CHRISTMAS

In the area of India south of Bombay, Christmas is celebrated by wearing new clothes, attending church, having a special meal, sending plates or trays of food to friends, and gifts in the family circle. Wandering groups of Christians sing carols on Christmas Eve and on into the early hours of Christmas morning.

Many homes are decorated with tissue paper festoons and strings of colored electric lights. Some Christians emphasize the use of colored paper lanterns. These may be of many shapes, but a star is the favorite. Fireworks, bought during the previous *Divali,* are sometimes set off on Christmas night.

Out in the villages people wear their new clothes and arrange a special meal to celebrate Christmas. Eating together is important as a sign of brotherhood in India. In addition to being a celebration for the Christians, this is an excellent opportunity to preach the gospel to non-Christians who gather to watch what is going on.—*Virginia McKenzie Parker*

EASTER

Good Friday services are observed where there are established churches and in some villages. In some places Palm Sunday may mean a parade with palm branches.

Very early on Easter morning Christians assemble for a sunrise service on a hill or at the cemetery. They return to the church, parading through the town when the sunrise service is finished. This service is often arranged by the women, and is often followed by other services during the day. At this time Christians greet each other with *"Jai Christ,"* "Victory to Christ."—*Virginia McKenzie Parker*

Pakistan

CHRISTMAS

The Christian children in Pakistan love Christmas just as children in North America do. Five or six weeks before Christmas, children begin to learn Christmas carols and frequently in *four* different languages. Many of them learn them in Urdu, the language most city children use; then in Punjabi, the basic language of the area but one used more in villages than in cities these days. Then many of the Christians remember the Hindi *bhajans* and they always enjoy singing them. Finally, they like to learn Christmas carols in English—the language also studied in most city schools.

Often the carol singing is accompanied by a variety of musical instruments. There is the harmonium, which is like a small organ, pumped with one hand and played with the other. There is a stringed instrument called the *sitar*. There is the flute; a pair of drums called *tabla;* a single drum, played with the palms of the hands; and sometimes cymbals as well as the violin.

Christians in Pakistan delight in decorating their houses for Christmas and getting pretty things to wear. Every church has a Christmas program, often with a young people's carol singing contest, the church school children's program, dramas, the Christmas tree from which gifts of clothing sewed by the ladies of the congregation are to be given to people in need.

But the biggest event is the congregational worship service on Christmas morning. Those folk who have spent most of the night of Christmas Eve cooking or going in parties to sing carols are not too tired the next morning to get to church. Even the children are brought to the service, which sometimes creates a cheerful hullabaloo. This is a great day in the life of Christians, and many people want their new babies baptized at the Christmas morning service. When the service is over, old friends embrace one another and others greet one another more formally. But one and all repeat the words, "May the great day be blessed."—*Mrs. J. M. Benade*

Philippines

BAPTISM

Birthdays may or may not be observed with a party in the Philippines, but baptisms always are. In the homes of both Evangelicals (as Protestants are called in the Philippines) and Roman Catholics, the baptism of a child is a time of great joy, and the parents happily celebrate the occasion by inviting many close friends—sometimes the whole church membership—to as sumptuous a dinner as they are able to provide.

Although the party is in honor of the infant or child, the children are trained to stay out of sight of the grownups, who undoubtedly fill the home to capacity. The children can be sure, however, that there will be

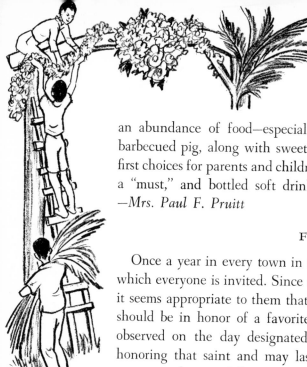

an abundance of food—especially the crisp browned skin of a whole barbecued pig, along with sweet rice and cassava cakes that are usually first choices for parents and children alike. Boiled rice, of course, is always a "must," and bottled soft drinks disappear in amazing quantity, too. —*Mrs. Paul F. Pruitt*

FIESTA

Once a year in every town in the Philippines there will be a party to which everyone is invited. Since most of the people are Roman Catholic, it seems appropriate to them that such an important and happy occasion should be in honor of a favorite patron saint. Thus the *fiesta* will be observed on the day designated by the Roman Catholic Church for honoring that saint and may last one day or several days. Since each town may have a different patron saint, *fiesta* days fall throughout the year.

Usually a large gateway constructed of wood and adorned with palm branches and flowers will be erected over the road at the entrances to the town. Lettering made of brilliantly colored flowers and green leaves pinned on the wooden structure may say "San Pedro" (Saint Peter), or if some important person is coming in honor of the *fiesta,* it might read, "Welcome Mayor Juarez and Party."

For many, the most important part of the *fiesta* may be the time of worship in the church. But for many others, the highlight is eating the delicacies which stretch every family budget. Traditionally, every home prepares food and stands ready to entertain any friends or relatives who come to visit. Since no one can be sure just how many will drop in, nor for how long, and since it is a humiliation to run out of food, great quantities of fruit, rice cakes, roast pig, broiled fish, baked custard, papaya pickles, cassava breads, coconut sweets, and often coconut or sugar cane drinks must be prepared. Just as turkey is the climax of much of our Western holiday eating, the barbecue-style whole roast pig is the favorite dish for special occasions in the Philippines. Children, and adults, too, like the crisp browned skin best of all.

Fiesta time, except for the church service, may have no special hours or program. It is a time for roaming the streets, shopping in the bazaars, visiting friends and relatives, and eating heartily.—*Mrs. Paul F. Pruitt*

CHRISTMAS

Christmas festivities among the Evangelical Christians in the Philippines usually center in church and school. In the rural areas the children will seldom have decorations or gifts in their homes. But in the Evangelical Christian churches, Christmas is a wonderful time, and the children anticipate it with great enthusiasm.

Often they prepare plays and pageants and they love to dress up in the way they think people of Jesus' day did. When palm branches and banana leaves are used in decorating the church, the result probably looks a lot more like Palestine than our Western churches do, with their holly and poinsettia. Especially in schools and homes in larger cities, Christmas is often observed with much happy construction of make-believe Christmas trees and also of lanterns made of gay-colored tissue paper. The lanterns may be constructed of bamboo and paper in the shape of a large star, with a lighted electric bulb inside, and placed on the porch in front of the house. The pretend-Christmas tree branches are made by twisting white or green crepe paper around tree branches or by winding them with many green brushes—like big bottle brushes—so that they look like pine trees. Other delights of the season include sharing food with neighbors, feasting on a meal of rice cakes, roast pig, salted eggs, sweets, and fruits.

On Christmas Day the children often go to the homes of their grandparents to pay their respects by kissing their hands and to receive gifts.

One of the things the little children love most about Christmas is the serenading that usually begins a week or two before Christmas and may continue several days thereafter. It resembles Hallowe'en "trick or treat" customs more than the serenading tradition. Groups of youngsters, from two or three to a dozen or more, go from house to house singing a carol or two and always singing as conclusion *"Maligayong Pasko,"* "Merry Christmas," to the tune of "Happy Birthday." At the finale, the home or store or business house serenaded is expected to acknowledge the greeting by giving the carolers money—a few pennies for children, or several dollars, if the group represents an officially sanctioned organization, such as a school, a church youth group, or a choir. Sometimes the children are in costume and accompanied by an instrumentalist, usually a guitarist, who will provide music for dancing.

In the larger cities, Western customs have been adopted in many homes, and a special Christmas dinner and family reunion are an important part of the festivities. But in the main, church programs are the most significant observance of Christmas among Evangelicals.—*Mrs. Paul F. Pruitt*

Sarawak

CHRISTMAS

On Christmas Eve, in Sarawak, a service is held in the church, which stands on stilts at the edge of the water. At its close the young people, dressed in white and carrying lighted candles, climb down the notched pole that leads to

the wharf below. They clamber into boats and paddle up and down the river, which serves as the village street. At the wharf of each member of the congregation, they stop and sing carols, ending with the greeting, *"Selamat hari Kristmas,"* "Merry Christmas." The householders are waiting for them and they set off firecrackers of every shape and size as their part of the ceremony. The singing goes on until midnight and then the young people return home for family celebrations.—*Judith Warren*

Taiwan (Formosa)

CHRISTMAS

In Taiwan, Christmas is celebrated among the Christians, who make up about five per cent of the population. The Christian community plans special programs for their churches, at which the children recite verses, sing songs, and even do little dances, interpreting the message of Christmas. The young people go caroling, making the rounds of the homes of the congregation, stopping outside their gates or windows, to sing and to give greetings. The church people make gifts for the lonely and unfortunate in jails, orphanages and institutions. There is little exchange of gifts between friends of families, except possibly an orange or toy for a child.—*Joyce Sutherland in Glad Tidings*

GREETINGS OF ASIA

BURMA

Mah-ya-lah?	Are you well (or strong)?
Mah-baa-deh	I am well

In a rural area the common greeting is to ask:

Be-ga-la-le?	Where are you from?
Beh-go-thwah-ma-le?	Where are you going?

This is not considered impertinent curiosity but expresses friendly interest.

When you go to visit at the home of a friend, the greeting at the door is, *"Win-bah-ohn,"* twice repeated, meaning "Come in, come in." As you leave, the host says politely, *"Nauk ta ka la ba ohn,"* meaning "Do come again."

CHINA

Ch'ih liao fan, may yō?	Have you eaten yet? (literally, but meaning Hello)

INDIA

Salaam	"Peace"

This greeting is spoken with a gesture of the right hand lifted to the forehead, and is used both as greeting and farewell.

Namaste	"I bow to you!"

This greeting is spoken with hands folded and lifted to the bowed forehead. It is proper for a younger person to greet an older person first.

Jai Hind	"Victory to India," used at the end of a speech
Jai Christ	"Victory to Christ," sometimes used by Christians

INDONESIA

Selamat pagi	Good morning
Selamat soré	Good afternoon
Selemat datang	Welcome (Prosperous coming!)

JAPAN

Ohaiyo San	Good morning (literally, Honorable morning)
Sayonara	Good-bye
Oyasumi nasai	Good night (literally, Honorably rest)
Banzai!	Hurrah!

KOREA

Ah lay nee chu mu sus so?	Good morning (literally, Have you slept in peace?)
Ah lay nee ka si o	Good-bye (Go in peace!)
Ussa, ussa, tu ru si o	Hurry, hurry, come in

PAKISTAN

Az salám alaikum	Peace be to you!
Wá alikum salám (reply)	And peace be to you
Khuda Hafiz	Farewell (God take care of you)

PHILIPPINES

Greetings in Spanish will be found on page 167.
Greetings in Tagalog follow:

Magandang umaga po	Good morning
Maligayong Pasko	Merry Christmas

: 4 :

Europe

FOLK FESTIVALS

England

BONFIRE DAY

Bonfire Day, or Guy Fawkes Day, is celebrated all over England on November 5. It commemorates the day in the reign of James I, in 1605, when a group of conspirators (one of whom was named Guy Fawkes) was narrowly prevented from blowing up the House of Parliament.

Today it is not wholly a children's festival, but it is the children to whom it particularly appeals and who make preparations for it. For days, even weeks, in advance, they take around a dummy, an effigy of the traitor, or a "guy," dressed in old clothes and wearing a mask, and ask passersby to give a "penny for the guy." They collect "chumps" (branches of trees, or any other pieces of wood) and store them for the bonfire. Rival groups of children compete to have the largest store of firewood.

On the evening of November 5, bonfires are lit in back

gardens or on open ground; the "guy" is placed on the fire, and fireworks are set off. It is here that parents come into the picture. Fathers supervise the tending of the fire and the lighting of fireworks. Mothers provide potatoes and chestnuts for roasting on the fire, and may also have made toffee and "parkin" (a kind of cake made from oatmeal, treacle, butter, and **ginger**) beforehand.

The weather on November 5 is often cold and damp, but most children go to bed happy, and extremely dirty, on that day!—*Constance Parker*

MAY DAY

In England the people are particularly fond of May Day—a festival that is celebrated all over Europe. May Day had its beginnings in a Roman festival of pre-Christian times, a festival held from April 28 to May 3 in honor of Flora, the goddess of flowers. At that time children decorated the columns of Flora's temple with garlands of flowers and danced before the flower-covered altar, singing joyous songs. Little clay images of the goddess were made for the occasion. With the coming of Christianity, the character of the festival changed but many of its customs remained. It became a festival in honor of the Virgin Mary and often little statues of the Virgin called "May dolls" were made at this time. The custom of gathering flowers and weaving them into garlands still remains.

When the festival is celebrated today it is usually held on the first Saturday of May. Flower garlands are used to decorate a large pole set up in the village. The youths and maidens of the village dance around it, holding the ends of garlands attached to the pole. Back and forth and in and

out they go, so that the garlands are twisted gaily round and round the pole.

In many countries, May Day is the time to go to the woods and bring back flowers and celebrate with song and dance. The New England Puritans frowned upon May Day customs and discouraged their observance. But it has survived as a children's festival, enjoyed throughout North America as well as in England.

Italy

CRICKET FESTIVAL

In Italy, and particularly in the city of Florence and its environs, there is a spring festival that is a great delight to children—the cricket festival. In former days when there were more gardens and open places in the city, people used to catch their own crickets, which are called *grillos* in Italy. At the present time, the crickets are sold in stores, confined in tiny painted cages made of wood or wire, each with a lettuce leaf to feed upon. The boys and girls have an exciting time selecting their crickets, which they then carry about to show to friends and relatives and to enjoy themselves.

The festival is a joyous one—the streets full of color and the shops selling balloons, toys, good food, and cool drinks. The crickets add to the festive atmosphere by chirping loudly in their cages. The children take their pets home and try to keep them alive as long as possible.

The custom of keeping crickets in cages seems to be an ancient one, since paintings of *grillos* in cages have been found on walls in Pompeii.

Scandinavia

MIDSUMMER

The Midsummer Festival is celebrated throughout Scandinavia and is held on the third week end of June. It marks the night when the sun never sets in the north of Scandinavia.

Early preparations consist of gathering the wood for the traditional Midsummer bonfire. Weeks before the festival, the children start to gather sticks and discarded wooden articles. There is often competition between families and villages for the biggest bonfire.

The festivities usually begin around noon on Saturday. Birch branches are set up beside doorways, and rooms are decorated with birch branches and flowers. In Finland, toward evening, the people go to the *sauna* for a steam bath.

Everywhere the people gather at the site of the bonfire. The women usually wear national dress. Just before or at midnight, the bonfire is lighted. The people play games or dance old folk dances around the fire, and this sort of fun may be kept up most of the night. All kinds of refreshments are served and enjoyed by the group around the bonfire.
—*Sister Pirkko Koskinen*

Scotland

HALLOWE'EN

Towards the end of October, the boys and girls of Scotland begin to look forward to the last day of the month, Hallowe'en. This name is popularly given to the eve or vigil of Allhallows, the festival of All Saints, which falls on November 1.

In the old Celtic calendar, this was the last night of the year, a time when witches were likely to be abroad. Later, when Christianity was introduced, the eve of Allhallows was taken over as a Christian festival and celebrated as the feast of the harvest; hence in present-day observances both fruit and vegetables play an extensive part.

Hallowe'en has long been associated with fun and revelry at the fireside; and with many ceremonies by young people of both sexes for divining a future sweetheart, for example, by dipping blindfolded into one of three bowls set before them. If a bowl with either clean, dirty, or no water is selected, the blindfolded person will marry, respectively, a spinster or bachelor, a widow or widower, or nobody at all. Nuts are burned in the fire to see if the couple will be happy or not. If the nut cracks or jumps, it is a bad sign; if it blazes or burns, it is a good sign.

Perhaps the two most popular observances for children are the eating, in semidarkness, of mashed potatoes in which trinkets have been hidden, and ducking for apples floating around in a tub or big basin of water. The person doing the ducking tries to catch an apple in his mouth, or tries to spear it with a fork dropped from his mouth or dropped from his hand held high above the bobbing apples in the basin.

The children may also dress up in old and borrowed clothes, and with blackened faces tour the streets, calling at people's doors. If the "guisers," as they are called, are invited in, they are expected to sing or to recite. In turn, they receive apples, candy, or some money. The children enjoy this part of the festival so much that they may spin out the calling for several nights during the last of October.—*Maimie Gavin.* (This festival is also celebrated in Canada and the United States. See page 122.)

CHRISTIAN FESTIVALS

Europe, Common to All

NEW YEAR

The New Year festival in Europe is derived from an old Roman celebration held in honor of the god Janus, who has given his name to the first month of our year, January. New Year's Day falls on the first of this month.

The early Christians changed the nature of the Roman feast. It became a time of fasting and a time of starting anew, leaving old errors behind. Over the centuries the fast was changed to a feast and the occasion became a time for merriment and for calling on friends. The making of noise on New Year's Eve comes from a very ancient custom of trying to scare away evil by noise.

In many countries of Europe families go to church on New Year's. In Denmark, at midnight on New Year's Eve, young people pound on the doors of friends, set off fireworks "to let in the new year." People roam the streets wearing masks and then go home to a special supper.

In Spain, it is believed that the luck of the coming year is settled by what happens on New Year's Day. It is thought that if you have plenty of good food to eat, you will have a prosperous new year.

In England, the father would gather his family around a bowl of hot spiced ale, called wassail, and each in turn drank some, giving New Year greetings. In the same country there is the custom of ringing muffled church bells before midnight. Then at midnight the muffles are removed and the bells ring out loud and clear. Thus the old year is "rung out" and the new year "rung in."

SAINT VALENTINE'S DAY

The fourteenth of February, Saint Valentine's Day, is a festival in honor of sweethearts. It is also a very ancient one, dating back to Roman times, when the Lupercalia festival was held on that day. Early in the Christian era, the festival was changed from the Lupercalia to one in honor of Saint Valentine, who was martyred on that day.

Many of the old customs were carried over to the new festival. The day was still celebrated as a special time for lovers, a time when young people sought sweethearts for themselves by means of magic. Sometimes this was done by having the names of young women written on slips of paper, each of which was then wrapped up tightly and dropped into a bowl. Young men drew out the names in turn and so selected a sweetheart for the year. Or a girl wrote boys' names on paper, wrapped them in clay and dropped them into a bowl of water. Many would sink but it was believed that her true love's name would float.

The custom of writing letters to one's sweetheart grew up and later it changed to the sending of pretty cards, with loving thoughts inscribed on them, often in verse—the Valentine card of today. This festival is also widely celebrated in the United States and Canada.

CARNIVAL

Before Ash Wednesday brings in the forty days of fasting and self-denial of Lent, there is held among most of the Roman Catholic peoples of Europe a time of revelry and feasting called Carnival, a word believed to derive from *carne vale* meaning "Farewell, O flesh."

In most places the festival is now limited to the Sunday, Monday, and Tuesday before Lent. During these three days pageants, parades, feasts, and other festivities, are held in the cities and villages. In Venice, Italy, a fat straw man, dubbed King Carnival, rides through the streets and rules until midnight of Tuesday, when his body, stuffed with fire-

works, is burned in a bonfire in Saint Mark's Square. In the streets a gay procession of people in costumes and masks pelt each other and onlookers with favors and candies.

In Germany and Austria, bonfires used to be set alight on hilltops and burning wheels were rolled down slopes to be quenched in streams at the foot of the hills. This was supposed to insure a good harvest and is probably part of an ancient festival.

SHROVE TUESDAY

In many countries of Europe, Shrove Tuesday, the day before Lent begins, is celebrated in special ways. It brings to an end the pre-Lenten celebrations that vary in character from place to place. It is a day of feasting on holiday foods that must be eaten up before Lent begins.

Pancakes and waffles are served in many households. In England, Shrove Tuesday is often called Pancake Day and there is a great deal of cooking and eating of pancakes prepared in fancy ways. In olden days, the "pancake bell" used to be rung, calling working people to stop their labors for a while and feast on pancakes.

In parts of the Netherlands, it is the custom on this day for people to eat a special kind of bread, in which is hidden tasty sausage meat, the last meat to be enjoyed until Lent is over.

In Denmark, Shrove Tuesday is a school holiday and a gay time for children. In the early morning the boys and girls go to their parents' bedroom carrying birch switches decorated with paper flowers, shouting, "Give buns, give buns." The parents then pass out from under the bed covers the tasty Shrovetide buns. Later the children may play games with the buns, hanging one by a string in the doorway or from a chandelier and trying to take a bite of the bun as it swings. The person who gets a nibble receives the bun.

In Norway, the customs are much the same as in Denmark. The children make a great effort to prepare switches of birch or evergreen

branches, tying them together with ribbons and decorating them with colored paper streamers or flowers. They go out early in the morning with the intention of switching all lazy people who are still in bed. They hope to receive a bun from every person they switch.

PALM SUNDAY

Palm Sunday is celebrated all over Europe on the Sunday before Easter. In general, the children's part in the service is the carrying of tree branches, usually palms, to the churches to be blessed, thus calling to mind the boys and girls who accompanied Christ on his triumphal entry into Jerusalem.

In some parts of Czechoslovakia, pussy willow branches are blessed in the churches and later carried to the fields to insure good crops, or are fastened to the roofs to protect the homes from ill fortune.

In Hungary, pussy willow branches are placed in the holy corners of the homes after being blessed in the churches; while in France, the palm branches are carried to the cemeteries after being blessed.

In parts of the Netherlands, the children make garlands of green leaves and fasten them on long sticks. These they carry from door to door during Holy Week, asking at each house for an egg for Easter. They collect a great many eggs in this way.

In sections of Yugoslavia, the people go to the river banks to get pussy willows and grasses which they carry to the churches, held aloft like banners.

EASTER

Easter falls on the first Sunday after the full moon, following the spring equinox. It is one of the great holidays of the Orthodox, Roman Catholic, and Protestant Christian Churches because it celebrates the resurrection of Christ. On the previous Friday, Good Friday, his death on the cross is solemnly remembered. On Easter Sunday, joy breaks forth as Christians rejoice in the risen Christ and feel assurance in his promise that they also shall rise.

As with many other Christian festivals, this special one has taken unto itself some of the rites and customs (such as the use of eggs) that were associated with an older observance at the same season, one celebrating the end of winter and the beginning of spring.

Easter is celebrated in most countries of Europe. Those who belong to the Greek Orthodox or Russian Orthodox Churches have a particularly impressive ceremony. Just before midnight on Easter Eve a procession forms in the darkened church which is draped almost entirely in black. The clergy wear their most gorgeous robes and march around the outside of the church. When the bell rings at midnight they march back into the church, carrying lights. The black draperies fall, the lights inside are lit and soon the church is ablaze with light. "Christ is risen," chant the priests. "He is risen indeed," the congregation responds joyously.

After the service the worshipers return home to feast on a bountiful Easter breakfast at a table decorated with flowers.

In Poland, the service is somewhat the same but takes place in the daytime.

In Germany and most other European countries, colored Easter eggs are given to the children, who are told that the Easter bunny laid them. It is believed by some that the custom of having eggs at Easter dates back to early Egyptian times.

On Easter Sunday almost everywhere people wear their new spring clothes, often vying with each other as to the splendor of their apparel. The churches are decorated with flowers on this day and the services are well attended and joyous.

SAINT JOHN'S DAY

Saint John's Day commemorates the birth of John the Baptist and is celebrated on June 24. Many of the customs associated with it were carried over from a festival celebrated for centuries throughout Europe on the same day—Midsummer Day. This ancient festival marked the summer solstice, when the sun is farthest from the equator. The old festival was marked by the building of bonfires and by the people dancing around them, jumping over them to insure good luck, by singing and feasting. In Scandinavia, the Midsummer Festival is still enjoyed. (See page 91.)

In Austria, on Saint John's Day, the young people build bonfires on hillsides and in fields. The country folk jump over them to insure good luck and good health. Boys dance around them carrying lighted torches.

In Germany, boys, girls, and young people go to open places and build large piles of wood, sometimes each bringing a piece. They eat a picnic meal and then Saint John's fire is set alight, as they sing old folk songs and dance around the blazing pile.

This festival is also celebrated in Czechoslovakia, France, and Hungary.

THANKSGIVING

The giving of thanks for a good harvest is one of the oldest and most widespread of festivals. It is celebrated on different dates in various countries and with varying customs but the idea behind all is the same— the offering of thanks for the harvest. With the recent upheavals in

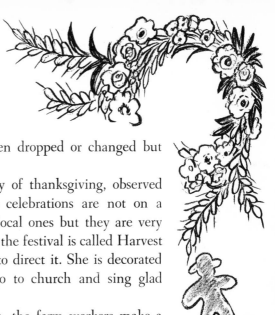

Europe, some of the customs may have been dropped or changed but it is probable that many still are observed.

Most countries of Europe set aside a day of thanksgiving, observed more in rural areas than in cities. These celebrations are not on a national basis; rather they are likely to be local ones but they are very old and very dear to the people. In England, the festival is called Harvest Home and sometimes a "queen" is selected to direct it. She is decorated with grain and fruit. The people often go to church and sing glad harvest songs.

In Czechoslovakia, when the crops are in, the farm workers make a wreath of wheat or rye decorated with flowers and put it on the head of the prettiest girl. After this ceremony a feast is held, and there is dancing. The food is usually roast pig or goose, and square cakes filled with plum jam.

In Germany, there also is a church and a field celebration. The last day of the harvest is given over to feasting and dancing, particularly barn and square dances. A large wreath of flowers is given to the local landowner and it is hung in a place of honor and kept until the next harvest. A feast follows at which gingerbread cookies, made in the shape of animals, hearts, and men are distributed to the people. In Hungary, much the same customs are followed. In Poland, at the time of the gathering of the crops people bring wreaths and bouquets of flowers to the church to have them blessed. Later they place them around their holy pictures at home. They also carry to the landowner a large wreath made up of grain and flowers to be hung up until the next harvest.

In Bulgaria, in the olden days, the last sheaf of grain from the field being harvested was called the Corn Queen and dressed in woman's clothes. It was carried aloft through the village heading a gay procession and then taken to a pond or stream and drowned. This was believed to insure plenty of rain for the crops of the next year.

CHRISTMAS

The festival of Christmas is the one that is most dear to the hearts of Christians, since it celebrates the birth of Jesus. There is no way of knowing with certainty when the birth took place. But tradition says it occurred during the season in which it is now celebrated and in the fourth century the reigning pope decreed that the Mass of Christ or Christmas should be celebrated on that day.

As with so many other festivals, Christmas took unto itself some of the ceremonies that had been connected with older festivals held in the same season. The Roman feast of Saturnalia, held in honor of the god Saturn, from December 19 to 24, came at the time of the winter solstice, when the days were shortest. It was kept as a season of merriment, feasting, decorating of houses, and the giving of gifts. It also celebrated the coming of longer days.

Northern people had a festival in honor of the god Thor, at which they burned Yule logs in their homes, as a way to insure good luck. In some parts of Europe, the Yule log is still burned in home fireplaces. In England, the mistletoe played a part in the ancient worship carried on by the druids, and mistletoe is used today in Christmas decorations.

The origin of using fir trees at Christmas is not clear, although many legends have gathered around it. One legend connects the Christmas tree with Martin Luther, but others place its use far back in the Middle Ages.

In many countries of Europe, Saint Nicholas is venerated at Christmastime. He was a real person, the Bishop of Myra, an old city in Asia Minor. He was always fond of children and many legends are told about his kindness to them and his love for them. His particular day is December 6, so he comes on the eve of that day, walking in the door after supper and leaving gifts as rewards for good children and telling the naughty ones they should be better.

Albania

CHRISTMAS

In the olden days in Albania, at the Christmas season, the table was set with a cloth, under which straw was laid, in memory of the humble birth of the Christ Child in a manger. The table was decorated with as many lighted candles as there were guests around it. It was loaded with good things to eat and the chief delicacy was a large cake, in which were many raisins and nuts and also a gold piece. It was believed that whoever found the gold piece would have good luck for the coming year.

Armenia

CHRISTMAS

There is no longer a separate country of Armenia but today many Armenians live in Turkey, the Middle East, Russia, and North America. Wherever possible, they carry out the beloved Christmas customs of their people.

Armenians follow the old style calendar and thus celebrate the festival on January 6 (or the Sunday following it, in the United States). Preceding it comes a week of fasting during which no meat, eggs, butter, or milk are eaten by the faithful.

On Christmas Eve, there is a supper of fish, lettuce, and spinach. Supper over, choir boys may go from house to house collecting bread, butter, wheat for *pilaff,* and other foods to be used for a large communal meal on Christmas morning. This will follow a service of worship in the church, to which ringing bells have called the people. Later in the day visits are made to various homes. The young people kiss the hands of older ones on whom they call, presenting gifts of fruit—oranges for women, and lemons for men. The children take gifts for their godparents—especially loaves of poppy seed bread, pastries, and roast chicken —and they receive from them gifts of money and new clothes.

The giving of gifts generally takes place at the New Year instead of Christmas, and on that day there is much feasting, merrymaking, and visits from the Armenian Santa Claus, called *Gaghant Bab*. There are special *Gaghant Bab* pastries, decorated with animals or birds or crosses. Candy is made of nuts, sugar, and grape juice boiled together, and in the evening the children sing and dance and are rewarded by gifts of candy and fruit.

Austria

CHRISTMAS

The Christmas festival in Austria lasts for two days, December 25 and 26, and is most beloved. On Christmas Eve the Roman Catholic families gather for dinners to which their relatives are invited. The chief dish for this meal is carp, since meat is not eaten at this time. After dinner, they gather around a pine tree, prettily decorated with ornaments, fruit, and cookies. A manger scene has a central place. Candy and cookies are served. The small children are put to bed and at midnight their elders go to attend Mass in the church.

On Christmas Day a big dinner is served at which the special foods are roast goose, ham, and fruitcake.

On December 6, the children receive their gifts from Saint Nicholas, who scolds those who have been naughty, and presents those who have been good with nuts, fruit, and candy.

Belgium

SAINT NICHOLAS' DAY

The most important day of the year for a Belgian child is Saint Nicholas' Day. It is celebrated on December 6, the birthday of Saint Nicholas, a long-ago Catholic bishop who was especially kind to children.

Saint Nicholas is portrayed in pictures as a tall, thin man with long white hair, dressed in the robes of a bishop and wearing a high, pointed hat. In his hand he holds a golden staff which is crooked at the end. He presents quite a contrast to jolly, plump Santa Claus. Saint Nicholas has a helper, a Negro named Nicodemus, who follows him, leading a donkey loaded with two large wicker baskets, called panniers, filled with candy and toys.

This celebration is reserved strictly for children. Beginning thirty nights before Saint Nicholas' Day, the child puts his two shoes in front of the chimney. This is repeated each night until December 5, and each morning the little one finds a caramel or a piece of hard candy from Saint Nicholas there.

On the eve of Saint Nicholas' Day, the child places his shoes before the chimney for the final time, and in each one he puts some turnips or carrots for Saint Nicholas' donkey, who must certainly be tired from carrying so many toys. Then the child sings:

> Saint Nicholas, friend of little school children,
> Bring me some sweets for my two small shoes.
> I will always be good like a little lamb,
> And I promise to say my prayers, in return for the candy.
> Come, come, Saint Nicholas, Tra-la-la.
> Come, come, Saint Nicholas, Tra-la-la.

Early the next morning, the little ones bounce from their beds to see what Saint Nicholas has left. The turnips and carrots are gone and in their place are toys and candy. Upon receiving their gifts, the children

stand before the chimney and say, *"Merci, merci,* Saint Nicholas," which means, "Thank you, thank you, Saint Nicholas."—*The Reverend and Mrs. Campbell D. Wallace*

Czechoslovakia

CHRISTMAS

December 24, in Czechoslovakia, is kept as a fast day and in many families the evening meal may be the first of the day. It is a very special meal, and its preparation has probably gone on for weeks. No meat is served at this meal, and fresh carp is often the main dish. There is also fish soup; several kinds of preserved fruit, nuts, candies, and cakes; and a special Christmas bread baked in fancy shapes and filled with nuts and raisins.

After the evening meal the family gathers around the Christmas tree and presents are given out. There is a custom of telling fortunes by pouring melted wax into cold water and foretelling the future by the shapes it takes. Sometimes the unmarried girls float in a dish of water some nutshells with tiny candles inside. The girl whose candle stays burning and upright longest will be the first to marry and will live longest.

At midnight the Catholic families attend Mass in the church, which holds the Christmas crèche and has been beautifully decorated with evergreens. Whenever possible, the celebration lasts for three days, December 25 and 26 being kept as holidays. Christmas Day is usually celebrated in the home with feasting and merrymaking.

Denmark

CHRISTMAS

Preparations for the Danish Christmas begin weeks in advance, with all the members of the family making presents for each other and helping to prepare the dough for the special Christmas cookies.

On Christmas Eve (*Juleaften*) the family goes first to church, then returns home for a dinner of roast goose, stuffed with apples and prunes, and served with red cabbage. An important part of the *Juleaften* meal is the *risengrød,* a rice pudding cooked with cinnamon and butter and hiding an almond. Whoever finds the almond in his portion receives a prize, such as marzipan. Danish children also set aside a large portion of the rice pudding, with an extra lump of butter in it, for the *Julenisse,* the Christmas elf who is believed to bring toys for good children.

Christmas Day is spent quietly at home or visiting friends. Hospitality is an important part of the Danish Christmas, and it is a tradition that no guest who enters the home during the holiday season should leave without eating or drinking, lest Christmas be carried away.

Eire (Ireland)

SAINT PATRICK'S DAY

March 17 is the anniversary of the death of Patrick, the patron saint of Ireland, and it is celebrated with great fervor. Patrick lived many centuries ago and it was he who brought Christianity to Ireland. Many legends are told about him, one of them being that he used a three-leafed shamrock to illustrate the idea of the Trinity. On his day the Irish delight to wear a green shamrock in honor of him. They have parades and speeches and a great deal of jollity. Country people in Ireland used to turn their cattle out to pasture and to plant their potatoes on March 17. (See also page 139.)

England

WHITSUNTIDE

Whitsuntide falls at the time of the Feast of Pentecost, the seventh Sunday after Easter. It recalls the time when the gathered disciples received the gift of the Holy Spirit. We may think of it as the birthday of the church. It used to be a favorite day for the christening of children, who were dressed in white robes for the occasion. During the Middle Ages, miracle and mystery plays used to be given at this time in order to spread the knowledge of the Bible. Everyone tried to have at least one new garment to wear.

The Whitsuntide holiday was celebrated in many parts of Europe. In Denmark and Hungary, "Whitsun kings" and "Whitsun queens" were chosen to reign for Sunday and Monday. In Spain, there was a procession to the church in which men, dressed as monsters and hobby-horses, took part.

Some customs observed on that day in England, such as the drinking of ale, morris and folk dancing, were carried over from an ancient festival held at the same time.

In the north of England, the Sunday and Monday of the Whitsun week end are used as opportunities for the churches to witness to the neighborhood. Local ways of doing this vary, the following description of a Whitsuntide Walk being limited to a small area of the West Riding in Yorkshire.

On Sunday afternoon there is a special service of singing and celebration, attended by old and young, all in new clothes for the occasion.

Monday is the great day, however, for this is the day of the "walk." After a short service in church, children and grownups form up in a procession outside. The minister and leading officials come first. Then come the children, arranged from the youngest to the oldest, with their

teachers, followed by the women of the church, in turn followed by the men.

The procession walks through the streets of the town. In the marketplace, it meets processions from other churches, and a brief open air church service is held. The streets are lined with people who may not themselves be attached to a church, though their children may be in the procession, which slowly makes its way back to the church, where tea is provided.

The traditional tea is a "long bun" (a light dough mixture containing currants and raisins), and two fancy buns. Whit Monday provides only simple pleasures, but for the children particularly it still is an occasion of very special joy.—*Constance Parker*

Finland

CHRISTMAS

In Finland, the celebration begins on Christmas Eve. After a steam bath, all members of the family join at a festival meal which consists of roast pork, rice pudding, homemade beer, and all kinds of vegetables and fruits. Christmas carols are sung, and children dance around the Christmas tree, often one they themselves have decorated. But the important event is the coming of Father Christmas. He usually delivers the presents personally, at least to children.

On Christmas Day, an early service is held in church at six o'clock in the morning. Otherwise the day passes without special activities. Then on Boxing Day, the first weekday after Christmas, people pay visits to their neighbors, and in the evening especially, young people gather to amuse themselves by playing games, dancing, and singing carols. A special custom, weather permitting, is to go out for a ride in a "one horse open sleigh."—*Sister Pirkko Koskinen*

France

THE FESTIVAL OF THE KINGS

In France, January 6 is a special day—the day many French families have a party to celebrate *La Fête des Rois,* the Festival of the Kings.

For days before January 6, pastry shop windows display *galettes* of all sizes. A *galette* is a round, flat cake about half an inch thick, made of layers of thin, flaky pastry. It can be the size of a dessert plate or as big as an oversized dinner plate. The important thing about a *galette* is that it has hidden in it a tiny china doll which plays a big part in the celebration. The doll represents the baby Jesus.

A party celebrating the day may include the family only, or guests may be present. There is one special moment toward the end of the party which everybody, especially the children, awaits with mounting excitement. This is the time when the *galette* will be served. When the moment arrives, the youngest person present passes out the pieces of the *galette*. Each person chews carefully on his piece. Then all at once there is a joyful exclamation—"I've found *le bébé Jésus* in my piece!"

The lucky finder is crowned king, *le roi,* of the festival, or *la reine,* the queen, as the case may be. He (or she) then chooses a consort to reign with him. If there are many people at the party, sometimes more than one doll is hidden in the *galette,* so that there are several kings and queens.—*Claire Hoffman Barth*

Germany

CHRISTMAS

Christmas celebrations usually begin early in December, in Germany, with the hanging of wreaths of evergreen tied with bright ribbon. Sometimes four Advent candles are attached to the wreath, one after another being lighted on each successive Sunday during the four weeks of preparation for Christ's coming. These are called Advent wreaths.

The Christmas tree idea is believed to have originated in Germany and practically every home has a lighted tree on Christmas Eve, around which the family gathers to sing Christmas songs.

Services are held in the churches on Christmas Eve and on Christmas Day. Crèches are set up both in churches and homes, and decorations of evergreen are seen everywhere.

As in many European countries, the German child expects gifts on December 6, Saint Nicholas' Day. In the evening he puts out his shoes and in the morning finds candies, nuts, and cookies in them.

The Christmas greeting is *"Fröhliche Weihnachten."*

Greece

CHRISTMAS

On Christmas Eve, carolers go from house to house in the village singing Christmas songs and receiving gifts of food or money. The special dish for Christmas dinner will probably be roast pig, if the family can afford it. The special greeting is *"Eti Pola,"* "A long life to you!" After dinner, there is music and dancing, and the giving of gifts to the children and to the poor.

One feature of the Greek Christmas season is the "blessing of the waters," on January 6, Epiphany. A high official of the Greek Orthodox Church, wearing his priestly robes, leads a procession of people, chanting songs, to the water front. There he halts and says a prayer, after which he hurls a cross into the water. Men and boys in nearby boats dive for the cross, which has a scarf tied around it. The one who finds it receives a special blessing from the priest and often a money gift from the bystanders.

Hungary

CHRISTMAS

As in many other countries of Europe, December 6 is the gift day for the children of Hungary. On the eve of the fifth, the children usually place their shoes in a conspicuous place, such as a window sill. Saint Nicholas, dressed in his bishop's robes and with a devil as a companion, is believed to pass by in the night. He leaves gifts for the good children and birch rods for those who have been naughty.

When the first star appears on Christmas Eve, the Christmas feast is served. Sometimes the family will gather around a Christmas tree and have a short prayer followed by the giving of gifts. The feast consists of cabbage soup, horseshoe-shaped cakes filled with walnuts and poppy seeds, special bread twisted into decorative shapes, and small dumplings covered with poppy seeds and sugar. A Christmas candy, something like fudge, is made and enjoyed.

At midnight the family goes to Mass in the Catholic church, which is decorated with greens. There is a two-day holiday. At Christmas time, the children also go along the streets dressed in their best clothes, singing carols and usually carrying a crèche with them.

Italy

CHRISTMAS

Among Italians, it is customary for families to gather for the Christmas Eve festival. The evening meal on that day must be meatless, but, nevertheless, a very special feast with very elaborate food. In some parts of the country, the women prepare twenty-four different dishes of foods for this meal.

It is usual for a Yule log to be burning in almost every home. In some places, before it is lighted, the children are gathered around it and blindfolded. Then each must recite a little verse to the Christ Child. When the blindfold is removed, the child finds before him some simple gifts which he is told the Christ Child has brought. In other homes, it is before the *presepio,* or manger scene, that the children recite their verses on Christmas Eve.

In certain parts of Italy, January 6, Twelfth Night, is the time for the giving of gifts. The *Befana,* an old woman wearing black clothes, carrying a broom and looking like a witch, visits the homes in the evening. She distributes presents to the children, putting gifts into the pockets of those who have been good and bits of charcoal into the pockets of the naughty ones.

The legend of the *Befana* recounts that long ago the Magi passed by the *Befana's* home, bearing their gifts for the baby Jesus. They invited her to accompany them on their journey, but the *Befana,* who was busy sweeping her home, said that she had too much work to do. Later, after she had finished her housework, the *Befana* took up her broom and started off down the road to Bethlehem. As she traveled she lost her way and was not able to find the baby Jesus. To this day, so the legend says, the *Befana* still wanders at Christmas time, seeking the Christ Child.

Poland

CHRISTMAS SUPPER

To Polish families, wherever they may be, Christmas Eve is the most beloved and most beautiful of all holiday observances. It is a time of forgiveness and love, of peace and good will.

The traditional *Wilia* supper, which begins as soon as the first star is seen on Christmas Eve, celebrates the coming of the Holy Child. It is a religious celebration, closely related to Roman Catholic family life, and a time when family members make every effort to be together. Grandparents, parents, and children, uncles, aunts, and cousins have a special feeling of family closeness and kinship. Many North American Polish families, who are not Roman Catholics, still observe *Wilia* customs simply because they want to be together and feel a close bond with past generations as they recall the years that have gone by.

The four weeks before Christmas are traditionally marked by fasting on Wednesdays, Fridays, and Saturdays. The day before Christmas is observed strictly as a fast day, and the *Wilia* supper is meatless. For days before, kitchens in Polish homes buzz with activity. Women prepare appetizers, such as pickled herring and pickled mushrooms; thick, creamy soup made of fish or fermented oatmeal and mushrooms; baked sauerkraut with yellow peas. They roll out and cut dough into small circles, folding into each a mixture of sauerkraut, cheese, plums, or prunes. These are the *pierogi,* which are cooked in boiling salted water, then served swimming in golden melted butter. There is fish, cauliflower, and buckwheat as well. And for dessert, there is fruit compote, poppy seed cake, nut pudding, pastries of all kinds, and coffee.

The food is served in courses, and tradition says that the number of courses must be seven, nine, or eleven, and that there must be an even number of people at the table. An extra place is set for the Holy Child, who may come to share in the *Wilia* as an unexpected guest or stranger.

According to a Polish proverb: "A guest in the home is God in the home." Straw or hay is placed under the tablecloth, as a symbol of the manger.

Before the meal begins, family members break with one another the thin sacred wafer, known as the *opłatek*, and wish one another the good things of life for the coming year. The *opłatek* is secured from the priest and is stamped with holy figures. Often, it is sent in a Christmas card to a relative or friend, as a symbol of love and peace.

After supper, the family join in singing *kolendy*, Christmas carols, which are an important part of the Midnight Mass, known as the *Pasterka* or Shepherd's Watch. *Kolendy* are sung throughout the Christmas season.—*Loretta Kruszyna Ingalls*

Scotland

CHRISTMAS

Christmas celebrations in Scotland are increasingly widespread. Places of business are closed. Children's or family services are held in the churches and last for a short period in the forenoon of Christmas Day. Very often the Christmas story is dramatized by the older boys and girls in the church or by young teachers.

The homes are decorated with colored paper, holly and other evergreens, and, of course, if there are young people about, some mistletoe hanging high in some obscure corner. More and more houses now set their Christmas tree at a window, where the lights may shine out on the streets, and some churches place Christmas trees at their doors.

Small groups of carol singers, carrying lanterns, gather at street corners or go to visit hospitals and charitable institutions.

On Christmas Eve, the children hang up their stockings—or something

larger!—or receive their presents at the foot of the tree. The children are also encouraged to give to the needy by bringing gifts, old and new, to special gift services at the church.

The traditional Scottish Christmas dinner consists of soup, then turkey, followed by plum pudding and mince pies. Families who may be living in various places are reunited, and old and young make merry together.—*Maimie Gavin*

EASTER

Easter week end is becoming more and more of a public holiday in Scotland, but in the churches, decorated with spring flowers, there are special services of praise. For the younger children, in many Sunday schools, small Easter gardens are made with moss and spring flowers, sometimes showing the figures of Jesus and Mary.

Most children receive Easter eggs of different kinds, either ordinary hard-boiled eggs which have been gaily decorated and colored, or those made from sweets. If the children live near an open space or park where there is a slight hill, they take their eggs out on the Sunday afternoon and roll them down the hill to symbolize the rolling away of the stone at Christ's tomb.—*Maimie Gavin*

Spain

CHRISTMAS

In Spain the little children look forward to the coming of Three Kings' Day, on January 6, when they will receive their presents. On the eve of the fifth, they place their shoes beside the door or on the balcony, and in them put some hay or straw or grain, as food for the animals that the Wise Men or Three Kings will ride. In the morning they find the food gone and in its place candies and gifts for themselves. (See also Christmas in Puerto Rico, page 151.)

Three Kings' Day concludes the Christmas festivities in Spain. On Christmas Eve, the families go to the Roman Catholic churches for Midnight Mass and when they return home a feast is served. Afterwards the family and their assembled relatives sing Christmas songs and rejoice together.

One special feature of the Spanish Christmas which the children particularly enjoy are the manger scenes, *nacimientos,* set up in various places. A great deal of imagination goes into the preparation of these little scenes, which may include besides the Holy Family, a donkey and a bull in the stable, and at a little distance from them, sheep, shepherds, and angels in one spot, and in another the Wise Men bringing gifts. The boys and girls gather around these scenes during the Christmas season and dance as they sing Christmas songs. The festivities last until Three Kings' Day.

Sweden

SAINT LUCIA'S DAY

The *Luciadagen,* or Saint Lucia's Day Feast, sometimes referred to as Little Christmas, *Lilla Jul,* is observed in Sweden on December 13, officially opening the Christmas festivities.

Lights are particularly associated with the *Luciadagen.* The explanation of this may lie in the derivation of the name, Lucia, from the Latin *lux,* or light. According to the old style calendar, this date was also the shortest day in the year and the turning point of the sun's light.

At the first cockcrow, sometime between one and four o'clock in the morning of December 13, the eldest girl in the family, preferably a blonde with long flowing hair, prepares to act the role of the *Lussibruden,* or "Lucia bride." She dresses in a white gown with a red sash and encircles her head with a wire crown wreathed with fir, whortleberry, or lingonberry twigs, and interspersed with seven or nine lighted candles

rising above her head. The "Lucia bride" goes from bedroom to bedroom, singing a special song to awaken the sleeping members of the household. She also serves them coffee or a sweet drink from a three-legged copper bowl, and round twisted saffron buns with raisin eyes in them, *lussekattor,* or "Lucia cats."

After everyone has arisen and dressed, breakfast is served in a room brilliantly illuminated by many candles. The people eat a sumptuous meal and they also serve special portions to the animals of the household.

From Saint Lucia's Day on, the baking of special Christmas cookies and cakes begins in earnest. Everyone, young and old, works together to prepare all the special food because the festival of Christmas lasts a month. Traditional Swedish hospitality will be shown to everyone who enters the home during this season and none may leave until he has partaken of some refreshments, lest he take the spirit of Christmas away with him. Thus, in Sweden, from Saint Lucia's Day on to January 13, there is one great Christmas activity and festivity.—*Muriel Carlson*

Sweden and Norway

FEEDING OF THE BIRDS

The Scandinavians are noted for their good food, and for their hospitality not only toward friends and neighbors but also towards animals and birds. These characteristics are particularly emphasized at Christmas.

Many of the customs go back to pre-Christian days and have since been approved by the church. The practice of giving the sheaf of the best grain to the birds seems to have sprung from the pre-Christian custom of making an offering from the harvest to the god of growth and fertility.

Today, in certain rural areas of Sweden, the householder selects and saves the largest sheaf of grain from the year's harvest. On Christmas Eve, accompanied by the children, he fastens the grain to the gable of

the roof or mounts the sheaf on top of a pole for the birds' Christmas feast. He then says words to this effect: "It's Christmas Eve; eat well, my friends." At this time of Christ's birth he wants all God's creatures to be cared for tenderly.

At Christmas time the children participate in all the advance work of cleaning, baking, and decorating the house—except for the Christmas tree itself which is secretly decorated by the parents. Since the Christmas festivities last a month, and since no person who enters a Swedish home during this season may leave without partaking of refreshments, there is a great deal of work to be done by everyone, and all enter into the spirit joyfully.—*Muriel Carlson*

Union of Soviet Socialist Republics—Ukraine

CHRISTMAS

In olden days, the Ukrainian churches, which were Russian Orthodox, celebrated their Christmas festival according to the old style calendar, so that their celebration came on our January 6. Christmas Eve was the most important family holiday observed by Ukrainians. It was rich in traditional rituals, stressing chiefly peasant customs combined with commendation of deceased relatives. The meal, called Holy Supper, consisted of twelve courses, in memory of the twelve apostles. Each family provided as bountiful a meal as it could afford.

Preparations for the supper began early in the morning when the housewife made a new fire in her large stove. She used for this purpose twelve pieces of wood which she had collected and dried for the past twelve days. With this fire she prepared twelve traditional meatless meals, using fruit and vegetables gathered from the family gardens and farm. The sequence in which meals were served varied and each section of the Ukraine kept to its own tradition. However, most of them included such dishes as beans, fish, stuffed cabbage, prunes, boiled wheat with honey, potatoes with mashed garlic, barley cereal with honey or oil, poppy seed cake, millet and corn cereal, and a fruit compote.

All day the family did no work except for preparing the meals. The head of the house made sure that everything was in order and that all members of the family remained at home and did not quarrel.

At night the head of the house brought into the house some hay and sheaves of wheat, barley, and rye and scattered them on the floor of the house, especially under the dinner table, while the housewife set the table. Under the table were placed various agricultural implements, or their parts. When the whole family was freshly washed and dressed in holiday clothes, they took their places at the table. The head of the house greeted those present and wished them happy holidays as they commenced their supper.

Some of the meal was shared with the animals of the household in their stables. After supper, some remains of the feast were taken to relatives and important people to show them that they were remembered.

The family also attended Mass in the Russian Orthodox Church. The Christmas festival lasted three days, and during that time carolers went from house to house singing, and the children often carried long poles with stars atop them.—*Mrs. Louise H. Kleopov*

GREETINGS OF EUROPE

DENMARK
Glaedelig Jul   Glad Christmas

FINLAND
Haushaa Joulua   Merry Christmas

FRANCE
Bonjour   Good day
Bonne nuit   Good night
Joyeux Noël   Happy Christmas

GERMANY
Guten Tag	Good day
Gute Nacht	Good night
Fröhliche Weihnachten	Merry Christmas

GREECE
Eti Pola	A long life to you!

ITALY
Buon giorno	Good day
Buona notte	Good night
Buon Natale	Merry Christmas

NORWAY
Gledelig Jul	Merry Christmas

POLAND
Dzień dobry	Good day
Dobranoc	Good night
Do widzenia	Good-bye
Wesoly Świąt Bożego Narodzenia i Szcześliwego Nowego Roku	Merry Christmas and Happy New Year (usually said together)

PORTUGAL
Boas Festes	Good holiday

SWEDEN
God Jul	Glad Christmas

: 5 :

North America

FOLK FESTIVALS

Canada and the United States, Common to Both

NEW YEAR

The New Year festival in both the United States and Canada comes exactly one week after Christmas, on the first day of January. It is a time for making a new start, for leaving behind old faults, for making resolutions to do better, to be kinder, to study harder, and so on. Also it is a time when the whole community has a gay holiday. (See also how the New Year is celebrated in Europe, page 93.)

The chief festivities come on the eve of the new year. Church-related families often go to a watch night service in the church to "watch" the old year die and the new year come in. It is a popular night for enjoying gay parties in homes and hotels, and for walking in the streets at midnight to listen to the bells, whistles, and sirens that greet the coming of the new year. Directly after midnight, friends and loved ones embrace and give each other the customary greeting, "Happy New Year to you!" and receive the reply, "The same to you!"

Those at parties or gatherings at this moment will often form a circle, holding hands, and sing a verse of the Scottish song "Auld Lang Syne."

In early days on this continent, New Year's Day was a time for calling at the homes of friends. Open house was held in the afternoon. All were welcome and a small feast of dainties was spread for the callers. This custom is still followed in some places.

BIRTHDAY

For a child, a birthday is almost the most important day in the year. It is the most truly his own of all the holidays. It is the day he is "king of the house" to the whole family.

"Happy birthday!" These the first words he hears in the morning are also the greeting he hears all day. Another form of greeting that is harder to bear but usually carried out enthusiastically by family and friends is the birthday spanking. The child whose birthday it is receives a spank for each year of his new age, and one more for good measure.

A birthday is a special day partly because of the birthday presents. The child may find them waiting for him at his place when he comes to the breakfast table. Or he may find instead a scrap of paper with a mysterious verse written on it—the first of a series of clues that will lead him on a "treasure hunt." The hunt ends when he comes to a present hidden in some unexpected place in the house.

The celebration of a child's birthday may be simple or

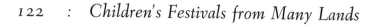

elaborate. It may be held for the family only, with a special dinner that includes all the child's favorite foods and is followed by a birthday cake with lighted candles. Or there may be a party, with other children invited as guests. They usually bring presents, too. There are games and refreshments, funny paper hats to wear and snappers to pull with a loud bang, so that they open up to show the prize inside.

The high point of the birthday celebration comes after dinner or toward the end of the party. It is the moment when the lights are turned off and the birthday cake, ablaze with candles, is carried in. As it comes, everybody sings, "Happy birthday to you!"

The cake is covered with decorations—sugar flowers and leaves and scrolls and usually a greeting written in icing. It holds tiny colored candles, the same number of candles as the child is years of age. The cake is placed in front of the birthday child. He makes a wish and blows out the candles. If he succeeds in blowing them all out in one breath, his wish will come true.

Then the cake is cut and pieces are given to everybody. Some families bake little favors in the cake, and there is great suspense until all these are found.—*Claire Hoffman Barth*

HALLOWE'EN

On the evening of October 31 Hallowe'en is celebrated, though some children manage to stretch the observance out to cover several of the preceding days as well.

The festival is of very ancient origin and includes many pre-Christian customs (see page 91). It was once believed that at that time the souls of the dead visited their homes and that witches, demons, black cats, and evil spirits were abroad. Many of the Hallowe'en decorations of today are holdovers from those old beliefs.

Today's Hallowe'en is particularly a festival for boys and girls, who dress in colorful or humorous costumes and troop about the streets with

faces daubed with paint or covered with masks. The little ones go out before dark and the older ones later. They move from house to house, knocking at doors, ringing bells and calling, "Trick or treat!" They usually receive gifts of food—apples, cakes, or candies—which they put into large bags for later feasting. Their tricks consist of marking on glass panes with soap or making noises on windows with tick-tacks.

Some children collect money for the Children's Fund of the United Nations, through UNICEF, instead of seeking treats for themselves.

A favorite decoration for Hallowe'en is a jack-o'-lantern, set in a window or on a porch. It is made of a pumpkin hollowed out inside and with eyes, nose, and mouth cut out so that a lighted candle inside shines through. Parties are often held at this time, particularly for older children. They play games traditional for this season, such as ducking for apples floating in a tub of water without use of hands, or trying to snatch a bite of an apple hanging at the end of a string with hands held behind the back. Another game is to try to pick up with the mouth a silver coin hidden in a dish of flour. Party food may be sandwiches cut round like pumpkins, cake with pumpkin-colored icing, and candies shaped like cats or witches.

Canada and the United States—Eskimo

RETURN OF THE SUN CEREMONY

Among some of the Eskimos, a ceremony is held when the sun appears on the horizon after the long weeks of darkness in the winter. The first day of the new sun must be greeted by fresh lights in the lamps. These are kindled from a fresh fire. So the children run from home to home, putting out the lamps that have lighted their igloos and homes throughout the days and nights of darkness.

WINTER FESTIVAL

In the far northland the Eskimos live in small villages, usually in family groups. Two or more groups may come together to celebrate a midwinter festival. They feast and dance and enjoy themselves.

The food for the festival may be seal or walrus meat. The dance is done to the beat of flat shallow drums made of hide stretched tightly over wooden frames. The drums are held by seated men who chant as they beat. The festival lasts as long as the food holds out. The children play together and often practice dancing off to one side.

There are likely to be games in which tossing will be a feature. In one, a large hide is held taut by a number of men. The jumper stands on this hide and is tossed into the air again and again. Often he rises high in the air. As long as he keeps upright he can jump on. As soon as he topples he must give way to another jumper.

Festivals from Foreign Lands

Most of the festivals celebrated by people living in Canada and the United States, in honor of the countries of their ancestry, will be found in Chapter 3, on Asia, and Chapter 4, on Europe. One holy day of people of the Jewish faith will be found under Israel (page 62), and two other Jewish festivals are given below, as celebrated on the North American continent.

Canada and the United States—Jewish Festivals

SUCCOTH

In late September or early October there comes a festival that Jewish children particularly enjoy. It is Succoth, a very ancient and happy festival. It is described in the Bible (Leviticus 23:39-43) and is also called the Feast of Tabernacles, the Feast of Ingathering, or the Feast of Booths. It began as a feast of autumn when the crops were safely gathered in and people were grateful for the harvest. It was also a time of remembering how the forebears of the Jewish people escaped from slavery in Egypt.

At the present time, the feast is kept by the family building a little booth of green branches, decorated with flowers and fruit, and placed in a garden, on a porch, or on a roof. A table is placed inside the booth and on it is a bowl of fruit in season, a dish containing citron and a sheaf of palm fronds fastened with myrtle and willow twigs. During the five to nine days of the festival the family eats their meals in the booth. They hold open house, entertaining their friends and relatives.

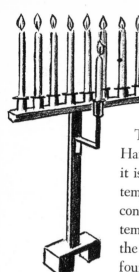

HANUKKAH

Toward the end of December, people of the Jewish faith celebrate Hanukkah, the Feast of Lights. It falls close to the winter solstice and it is a happy festival. It celebrates the cleansing and rededication of the temple in Jerusalem, after it had been freed from occupation by an enemy conqueror, years before the Christian era. Legend reports that when the temple had been cleansed and the light that had always burned before the altar was to be rekindled after being dark for many years, it was found that there was but one small flask of oil at hand, a supply that would last only one day. The lamp was lit and miraculously it burned for eight days, until a fresh supply of oil was procured.

Today, the festival lasts for eight days and lights are its special feature. The eight-branched candlestick, *menorah,* has a special place in the home. The candles are lit by the man of the household, one extra for each day; that is, one on the first day, two on the second, three on the third, and so on. Praise is given to the Lord for saving the Jewish people from their enemies. Much is made of this ceremony and the traditional decoration is the six-pointed star of David.

Gifts are wrapped in blue and white paper. The children receive new coins and other gifts. They play Hanukkah games, particularly one with a square top. Good food is served and everyone is very gay.

Canada—Nova Scotia

APPLE BLOSSOM FESTIVAL

How would you like to go to an Apple Blossom Festival in the Land of Evangeline? Such an event is held each year in the lush Annapolis Valley of Nova Scotia. The festival usually takes place early in June when the apple blossoms are at their best. It lasts for a week end, during which time the air is filled with the scent of blossoms and fresh-growing

things. In character it resembles the Apple Blossom Festivals held in apple-growing regions of the United States.

"Princesses," usually teen-agers, selected from each of the towns around, attend a tea and reception held at the Cornwallis Inn in Kentville, Nova Scotia, on Friday afternoon. The public has a chance to meet them there, and judges, who remain unknown, mingle with the crowd to choose a "queen." In the evening, at a dinner and dance, the queen is announced.

On Saturday morning there is a junior parade in which many children wheel decorated doll carriages, and children's choirs participate. The grand parade on Saturday afternoon features about twelve floats from the various Valley towns, and each year there is a theme for these floats. One year it was "Legends." Dances are held in several of the towns on this night.

On Sunday, people may attend public worship services and later view the floats which are set up in a grand parade park.

This festival, begun in 1933 as a means of publicity for the beautiful Annapolis Valley of Nova Scotia, has now become a traditional festival.
—Ella Des Brisay

HIGHLAND GAMES

Highland Games are held for two days each summer in the town of Antigonish, Nova Scotia. Their origin dates back to 1861, when a Highland Society was formed for the purpose of preserving "the martial spirit, language, dress, music, games, and antiquities of the Caledonians; for relieving distressed Highlanders at a distance from their native homeland; and for promoting the improvement and general welfare of our native country."

At the opening of the games a brief ceremony is usually conducted by some important person in civic or provincial government life. Traditionally, Highland Games are opened with the ancient Gaelic welcome,

ciad mile failte, "a hundred thousand welcomes." A few speeches are made, and the games are declared open.

Although not a children's festival, the youngsters get a great thrill out of the gatherings. They compete in the reels and step-dancing, and some quite small children have a "go" at the bagpipes. The competitions are carried on from morning to night in order to give every contestant an opportunity to take part. Special playground facilities are provided at the site of the festival.

Along with the sword dances, highland flings, reels, and bagpipe contests, there are all kinds of track and field events so that everyone has an opportunity to participate.

One of the traditional Scottish sports is tossing the caber. A caber is the heavy trunk of a tree from sixteen to twenty feet long. It must be tossed so that it turns over in the air and lands away in a straight line. The winner is the one who tosses in the best and most easy style, and whose caber lands in the straightest line.

Pugwash, and St. Ann's, as well as other areas in Canada and in the United States, also have Highland Games each year.—*Ella Des Brisay*

Canada—British Columbia

INDIAN POTLATCH

In the olden times, before they adopted white men's ways, the coastal Indians of British Columbia (and other coastal tribes farther south, such as the Yakimas) used to gather in the midwinter for *potlatches.* Each tribe, consisting of families related in some way, usually held its own celebration in its own "long house"— a structure built of cedar logs and one hundred or more feet in length. Around the inner wall of the house was a bench, about two feet high and five feet wide.

Each family attending the *potlatch* was assigned a section of this

bench for its sleeping quarters, and in front of that section the family set up its cooking kettle.

A *potlatch* celebrated some special event, such as the giving of a new name to a child. Of course, every child was given a name at birth. But as the child increased in size and skills, he (or she) was given a new name, a special name of his own. This ceremony of name giving around the time of puberty was common to most Indian tribes.

In preparation for the *potlatch,* which would bring him a more impressive name, the child collected presents, not for himself but to give away. His parents collected much food and invited the families of their tribe to the gathering.

As festivities began, the important men rose to make speeches about the child, who stood listening gravely—and silently. As each speaker ended, the boy gave him a present, possibly a blanket. After the speeches, a group of men and women came in and performed a ceremonial dance, sometimes singing new songs they had made up. Next came the feast. The host provided fresh or dried deer and bear meat and salmon. These were boiled in and eaten from the family kettle. The festivity went on as long as the food lasted and often the family gave away all its assets.—*Muriel Millen*

Haiti

NEW YEAR

January 1 is an important holiday in Haiti, because it combines New Year's Day with Independence Day, the day when the Haitians finally revolted from the French. On this day, fireworks are set off in the cities. Even the

poorest people make a big effort to have a new dress or shirt or suit to wear on that day. They believe that whatever happens to them on January 1 is a sign of what will happen during the year. Therefore, they like to wear new clothes, give and receive gifts (especially money), and visit their friends, in the hope that these pleasures may be enjoyed throughout the year. The day is spent in feasting, visiting, and making merry in general.—*Mrs. Harold Heneise*

Trinidad

DIVALI

About the first of November, the many Hindus who live in Trinidad usually celebrate the Feast of Lights, *Divali,* which they brought with them from their native India.

For the festival, the Hindus buy little pottery lamps, or *duyas,* which are placed around the outside of the house, on window sills, down steps, and on gallery railings. Each little *duya* is filled with coconut oil, and a bit of twisted cotton is placed in it for a wick. As soon as it is dark, the children are allowed to light the tiny lamps. It is a wonderful sight to walk down a street and see the house outlined with the lights. The boys and girls keep running about to make sure the lamps stay lighted. Later, everyone joins in a big feast. As the older Hindu men and women come into the house for the feast, they will fold their hands together, bow their heads and say, *"Sitaram, sitaram,"* in greeting.—*Constance Wagar* (See also page 52.)

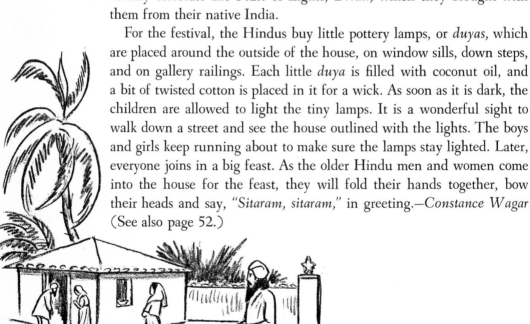

Mexico

FIESTA

The *fiesta* is a community holiday enjoyed by Mexican families in the area in which it takes place. A *fiesta* is not limited to Mexico, however, but is celebrated throughout Latin America. It may be held in honor of a saint, a religious holiday, or a national holiday. From youngest to eldest, all rejoice in the *fiesta*.

The celebrations may begin at dawn, with the noise of rockets firing and the ringing of church bells. Little booths are set up in the central plaza and these burst forth gloriously with colored tissue paper streamers. Gay packages filled with candy and wrapped in fringed paper, brilliant cakes, and tempting drinks make their appearance; and delightful toys with special souvenirs for this *fiesta* are piled on the booths.

The mask vendor appears at every *fiesta* and for a few *centavos* anyone may buy a gaudy paper mask and thus turn himself into a grotesque animal, a beautiful fairy, or an ugly devil.

In large towns a street fair adds to the excitement, with its squeaking merry-go-round and Ferris wheel. Above the music of bands and the voices of strolling musicians rise the cries of barkers, who with drums and trumpets try to induce people to come into the tents where actors, dancing or singing on miniature stages gaudily decorated with painted scenery, hold the audience spellbound.

The antics and quarrels of the *fantoches,* the Mexican Punch and Judy, are always greeted with shouts of laughter. The marionettes, little clay figures on wires, have a wide repertoire and their lines are spoken by ventriloquists.

No *fiesta* is complete without fireworks, and the skilled craftsmen of this art, who have added the imagination of the Indian to the craft learned from the Spaniards, can produce wonderful animals filled with roman candles, which burst while being carried. There are many special

dances, each fitted to the occasion that is being celebrated. Favorite costume for the women is the *china poblana,* and for the men, the *charro.*—From *Over the Mexican Border,* by Mildred Hewitt. New York, Friendship Press, 1935.

PIÑATA

A *piñata* party may be held at Christmas time, on somebody's birthday or name day (saint's day), on the last day of school or vacation school, or at any time there is a party for children. *Piñatas* are always great fun and are very popular with little folk in Mexico.

The party usually begins with some lively games. Then the *piñata* is brought out and admired. For, of course, the *piñata* itself is the most important thing at this kind of party.

A *piñata* is a cheap pottery cooking jar, filled with goodies and decorated with construction paper, crepe paper, or tiny curls of tissue paper, so that it looks like a flower, a ship, a plane, a clown, a donkey, a star, a child, an elephant, or almost anything you can imagine.

The *piñata* is hung on a long rope, the ends of which are held as high as possible, by two people, standing on a roof or a wall, if the *piñata* is outdoors. If it is indoors these two people stand on chairs, pulling the rope taut or letting it down low alternately, trying to keep the *piñata* from being broken.

The children take turns being It, practically always beginning with the smallest ones. The one who is It is blindfolded, given a long stout pole, and is turned around three times, then is turned loose to break the *piñata* if he can.

How everyone laughs when he goes in the wrong direction! How they shout, "Over here!" or "Higher!" when they try to help him! When the *piñata* is finally broken and the goodies fall out, everyone scrambles to get his share. Such a pile of children as usually results!

Sometimes several *piñatas* are broken in one *fiesta*.

If you want to make a *piñata* in a land where there are no cheap pottery jars, just fill a big paper bag with unshelled peanuts or with wrapped candies, tie it tightly, leaving a loop to put over the rope, and then decorate it as you wish.—*Mrs. Ella H. Kepple*

United States

MAY BASKETS

With the approach of spring the children of New England look forward to May Day. Originally an old Roman holiday dedicated to the goddess Flora, May Day has persisted through the ages in one form or another (see page 89). At one time it was extravagantly celebrated in England. Celebration of the holiday continued despite the disapproval of the stern Puritans, who frowned upon its pagan origin and thought it "too frivolous" for their sober children. Gradually it emerged and continued in New England in more modest versions as a simple exchange of May baskets on May 1.

May baskets can be bought or made, for the shops at this season carry them in all sizes, colors, and prices. But most children make their own, spending many happy hours beforehand in their preparation.

The method is simple. Small boxes, paper cups, or even cornucopias, made by rolling a sheet of paper to the desired size and pasting the edges together, are covered in various ways with fringed tissue papers or crepe paper with edges carefully fluted. Handles, of course, are added. The boxes can be decorated in all sorts of ways so the possibilities are endless and it is a wonderfully satisfying experience for a child.

Delivering the baskets is fun, too. On May 1 the baskets are filled with candy and fresh flowers. Wild flowers are best, if the environment and season permit; if not, anything the child can get. The basket must be left on the doorstep of the favored friend, or hung on the doorknob; the bell is rung with gusto, and the donor skips away before he can be "caught." This is the "proper" way. But occasionally a child may hide, not too successfully, in the shrubbery, obviously hoping to be seen and identified with some particularly noble creation. And occasionally there will be a receiving child so materially minded as to look first at the size of the basket and the amount of candy he gets. But it is all part of the fun.

May Day means far more than just another celebration, and a child who has participated in this May Day rite can never forget it. It becomes something he will remember nostalgically every year—something beautiful, allied to spring and one of its symbols, along with pussy willows, and the piping of spring frogs at dusk.—*Mrs. Edwin Marble*

United States—Hawaii

Hawaii rejoices in a mixture of races such as is found nowhere else in the world, and they live together in harmony and friendliness. Many groups still keep to the customs of their ancestors' homelands. The Chinese community celebrates the Chinese New Year (see page 46). The Japanese community keeps *O Bon Matsuri* (see page 66) and Girls' Day and Boys' Day (see pages 64 and 65). But a number of the festivals, such as Lei Day and Aloha Week, celebrated today by people in Hawaii sprang from the customs of the native Hawaiians.

LEI DAY

Lei Day falls on May 1, a time when there are plenty of fresh flowers. It was instituted in 1928 and is a day for showing friendliness. Nearly everyone wears a *lei,* a garland of flower heads threaded on a string with the ends tied together. There are special programs in the schools and tales of old Hawaii are told. There are contests with prizes for the most beautiful *lei* and the best ones are put on display. Some of the garlands are made completely of unusual orchids. Everyone is always cheerful and smiling on that day.

ALOHA WEEK

In October comes an important week-long festival, lasting from one Sunday to the next. It is Aloha Week and it began officially in 1947. It is a time for remembering the early history of Hawaii. Pageants are presented in the parks depicting scenes from that history. The most colorful event is the arrival over the water in separate canoes of the "king" and the "queen." The king wears a helmet and a gorgeous cape, as did the royal leader of old, and the queen has a bevy of beautifully dressed attendants. In the ceremony that follows some of the old *hulas* are danced.

United States—Indian American

BUNNY DANCE FEAST

The Bunny or Rabbit Dance Feast was one engaged in by the boys of the Plains Indian tribes and it is still enjoyed today. It is intended for boys from six to ten years old, although their little sisters often join in the dance.

On some bright day the dance begins. To the beat of a drum the boys pretend to hop like bunnies. They move their two feet together in a hop as a rabbit does, or they hop from one foot to another in one of the usual Indian dance steps. As they hop, the boys put their hands to their heads above the ears, the thumb inward and the fingers open, and flap their "bunny ears" in time to the music. They move in a line, always keeping in step with the music. The small girls often join the end of the line

and dance in little short steps from side to side, the usual Indian women's dance step.

The parents watch the dance proudly and at the close of it give a feast they have prepared for the children.

GREEN CORN FESTIVAL

This festival was held in the past by Indian tribes that grew corn as part of their food supply, notably the Iroquois and the Cherokee. It was held when the green corn was ready to eat, usually in August, and lasted for several days.

The festival began with the chief sprinkling tobacco over the coals of a small fire and making a prayer of thanks for the gift of corn. Then began a dance by the men, to the beat of drums and accompanied by chanting. Clowns in masks carried on amusing antics.

Among the Indians the dance was serious and had a religious meaning, though it could also be warlike or comic. The dance had a set form and the steps were carefully prescribed.

The boys and girls watched the dancing and sometimes joined in by forming separate circles of their own. In the evening came a feast of newly cooked fresh corn at which everyone ate to his heart's content.

MAPLE FESTIVAL

This was a festival that was once held by the Iroquois Indians—an important one because it had to do with food. It took place in the early spring, sometime before the snow was off the ground, when the sap began to run in the maple trees. The tribal council selected a day when the tapping of the trees was to begin.

In the morning the people went to the maple groves and before beginning to tap the trees held a service of thanksgiving to the trees for giving them the "sweet water" for their food. The tribal chief built a small fire under a large maple tree and sprinkled tobacco leaves over its red coals, at the same time giving thanks and asking protection for his people. The men formed a circle around the big tree and moved about it solemnly, singing a chant and shaking their rattles in time to the beat of a drum. The women formed their own circle outside the men's and moved in their own dance step.

After the dance, the men tapped the trees, cutting slits in the bark and slipping little wooden spouts into the slits. The women put containers under the spouts to catch the sap. While the sap was being gathered and boiled to syrup over slow fires, the company played games and generally enjoyed themselves. After the games, came a feast of cornbread and newly made maple syrup. The Chippewa Indians also had a Maple Ceremony at which the medicine man sang a special song, the words and music of which may be found in *The Whole World Singing*.

RAIN DANCE FESTIVAL

Among the Hopis and the Zuñis and other agricultural tribes living in the desert areas, rain was very important. Therefore, the tribes held ceremonies and dances which they hoped would insure an adequate supply of rain for their crops.

The men of the tribe dressed up for the dance by painting their bodies in bright colors and wearing strings of beads and silver ornaments that rattled as they moved. They also carried rattles made of dried gourds filled with pebbles, these having been inserted through a hole into which a length of corn stalk was later thrust to serve as a stopper and a handle. Sometimes the men wore turtle shell rattles tied to their legs, so that with every move they added to the music produced by the drums.

The ceremonies were usually directed by a number of priests wearing false black beards and white cotton kilts, and carrying spruce twigs. A

clown supplied the comedy, wearing over his head a sack with a face painted on it. He carried on all sorts of antics to amuse the watching crowd, falling down, hopping about, getting in the way of the dancers. The dancers, however, were serious as they moved along in a line, singing the rain dance song, and stamping hard with their right feet. The stamping, the shaking of the rattles, and the singing gradually grew louder and louder. Meanwhile the head priest made motions of dipping up water and the dancers imitated him. When the dance reached its climax, there were loud yells and shaking of rattles as it came to a sudden end.

CHRISTIAN FESTIVALS

Canada and the United States, Common to Both

SAINT VALENTINE'S DAY

This is a day for sending pleasant messages to friends and sweethearts, often with no name signed, so that the receiver must guess who the sender is. At this season the stores are full of lacy, dainty valentine cards, sometimes with verses of love and friendship written inside. Some children prefer to make their own, however. Red hearts and cupids are a favorite picture theme on the cards.

In the schoolrooms, particularly in the lower grades, there is often a red and white valentine box, into which cards are dropped by the pupils, often unsigned. Each child hopes to get many pleasant surprises when the box is opened and the cards are passed around.

The day is a favorite time for parties, with red hearts and cupids as the decorations. Cakes and sandwiches may be in the shape of hearts or decorated with them. Fortune telling games are popular and sweethearts are chosen. (See page 94 for origin of festival.)

SAINT PATRICK'S DAY

On March 17 comes the celebration in honor of Saint Patrick, the patron saint of the Irish. Everyone with Irish blood takes some part in it.

Tradition has it that Saint Patrick brought Christianity to Ireland in the early days. There are many colorful legends about the good things he did for that country and he is much beloved. (See also page 105.)

March 17 honors the anniversary of his death. In North America, in places where there are many Irish, March 17 is celebrated by big parades and by wearing "something green"—often a piece of green cloth cut in the shape of a shamrock.

EASTER

All Christian people keep the spring festival of Easter, which celebrates the resurrection of Christ (see Index). Easter falls on the first Sunday after the full moon following the spring equinox and the date may vary from late March to the third week of April.

At Easter time, the churches are decorated with flowers, Easter lilies being favorites. New spring apparel is worn to special worship services which are observed in the churches at this time, and Easter hymns are sung joyously. Open air services early on the morning of Easter Sunday are being held more and more widely every year, and are heavily attended.

The custom of hard boiling, coloring, collecting, and giving Easter eggs delights the children at this season. Candies shaped and dyed like colored eggs and chocolate bunnies are on sale in the stores at this season. It is the custom in the United States for the President and the First Lady to entertain children on the lawn of the White House at Easter time. A band plays and the children roll their eggs on the lawn to celebrate the rolling away of the stone from Christ's tomb.

The Moravian church in Winston-Salem, North Carolina, has an outstanding Easter service. Just before dawn the musicians go to the

Moravian church, where a crowd has gathered, for cake and coffee. A short service follows and then a procession forms, with the clergy at the head and church members and visitors behind. All march to the cemetery, where the white gravestones have been washed and decorated with flowers. From the corners of the cemetery the bands play antiphonally, "Jesus Christ Is Risen Today" and a joyous Easter is observed.

CHRISTMAS

For Christians, Christmas, meaning Christ's Mass, is one of the great celebrations of the year and for children unquestionably the greatest. At that season, homes are decorated with greens and colored lights; wreaths are hung on front doors; and an evergreen tree is purchased to be set up and made gay with colored balls, tinsel, and a variety of pretty ornaments, cherished and hoarded from year to year.

In many homes it is the children's responsibility and delight to decorate the Christmas tree and they may make a rite of it, lifting with care each beloved ornament from the box in which it has lain for a year, and placing it at an advantageous spot on the tree, often after many trials. A shining star usually adorns the very top of the tree, fastened there with adult aid, if necessary. Some children help in trimming the house and even aid in making the wreath for the door. Sometimes a crèche is set up beside the tree.

For days, perhaps for weeks, children have been making or purchasing gifts for their brothers and sisters, parents, relatives, and friends, almost exploding with the burden of the delightful secrets they carry. Now the gifts are wrapped in colored paper and laid on the tree or under it. Christmas Eve is usually spent in the home, where there may be carols sung around the piano or Christmas stories read or told. Relatives may have already arrived, since the festival is a time of family get-togethers.

The younger children are wildly excited over the expected visit of Santa Claus, a cheerful, chubby fellow dressed in a bright red suit

trimmed with white, who is believed to distribute gifts to good children in the early morning of Christmas. Older children are more sophisticated but are almost as full of excited anticipation as the little ones. It is with difficulty that the children are persuaded to go to bed. Early the next morning, often before dawn, they waken and rouse the household.

In some homes, stockings are hung up to receive gifts, one for each member of the family who is present. Sometimes stockings are hung on bedposts so that the children can get them the moment they waken and find a few gifts— some candy and nuts and an orange or apple in the toe. Sometimes the stockings are hung along a mantelpiece.

Customs vary in different families, some having the stocking gifts before breakfast, others going to the tree first. And what a sight that tree is, with its colored lights glowing, its bright ornaments shining, and its gifts piled on and under its branches! Father, or some chosen person, hands out the presents in turn and happiness reins. Later in the day there is a big Christmas dinner for all the assembled family, with roast turkey and cranberry sauce, mashed potatoes and squash, mince pie or plum pudding as the favorite foods. The tree and the decorations are usually kept in place until after the New Year festival.

Christmas is a special time in the churches too. They are decorated with evergreens and sometimes blooming flowers such as poinsettias. In many churches a special service is held on the Sunday just preceding Christmas, and the church glows in the light of candles or electric bulbs shaped like candles. The choir sings especially rehearsed carols, the Christmas story is read from the Bible,

and everyone remembers with joy and reverence the Christ whose birthday it is and in whose honor the festival is being held. Carols are sung in the churches all during this season. Many congregations hold a midnight service on Christmas Eve which is attended by devout families.

Canada

THANKSGIVING

In Canada, Thanksgiving Day has long been celebrated because early settlers from Europe brought the custom with them (see page 98). The holiday falls on the second Monday in October. It is a time for family get-togethers and for enjoying a feast. The traditional foods are roast turkey, fresh vegetables, cranberry sauce, and fruit. The first time Thanksgiving was celebrated as a national holiday throughout the dominion was on October 9, 1879. Sunday church services usually center around the theme of Thanksgiving.

French Canadian

SAINT JOHN'S DAY

June 24, Saint John's Day, is celebrated all over French Canada. In the country parishes, there are usually races, games, booths, candy and other good things for sale, church dinners, and much general merriment.

In the cities, parades are held, with floats depicting the historical highlights of French Canada. Children attend the parade in large num-

bers and learn some of their peoples' history as they watch. Prizes are given for the best float.

Montreal has a spectacular parade which moves along one of the principal streets of the city from which all traffic is barred for a time. The most important feature of the parade is the float on which is a little boy dressed as a shepherd of old, representing Saint John as a child, and with him on the float is a pet lamb, all woolly white and with a ribbon and bow around its neck. Great crowds watch the parade and cheer little Saint John and his lamb.

SAINT CATHERINE'S DAY

In French Canada on November 25, there falls Saint Catherine's Day. She was a virgin martyr and she is the patron saint of unmarried women. In Europe part of the celebration of her day was the setting off of fireworks shaped like little wheels that turned and sputtered out showers of sparks—the Catherine wheel. The young people gather in homes on November 25, to enjoy good times, one of the popular features being a taffy pull.

CHRISTMAS

French Canadians call Christmas Eve *Nuit de Noël*. The family goes to Midnight Mass, which is followed by a special supper at home. Favorite foods are various pork dishes, roast turkey, ragouts, fruit, plum pudding, pastries, nuts, and candy. The children hang up their stockings for Père Noël, or Saint Nicholas, to fill.

The holiday season lasts until January 6, with parties in the homes and social gatherings. On the final day, *le Gateau des Rois,* the Cake of the Kings, is baked, with a pea and a bean in it. The lucky finders of the pea and bean respectively become the king and the queen of Twelfth Night.—*Yvonne Gignac*

Central America

FEAST OF THE PATRON SAINT

The day in which the patron saint of the town or village is honored by the *fiesta patronal* is a time of great celebration. Houses in the village or town are cleaned and repaired and, if possible, repainted or white-washed. The streets are cleaned and the potholes mended. Those who can afford them buy new clothes, or make costumes for the festive day.

The country people come to town from miles around to see the sights of the festival, to sell their produce, and to go to Mass in the church. There are singing, dancing, games, and often puppet shows and merry-go-rounds for the children. Music is played continually.

In Panama, the *fiesta* often includes cockfighting, bullfighting, and gambling. In the towns of Panama the women often wear on the *fiesta* day costumes called *pollera,* made with much embroidery and yards of lace. Their hair ornaments are in the shape of flowers and butterflies.

In Guatemala, every village has its own *fiesta patronal,* which may last for days. One popular musical instrument there is a marimba made of gourds. At the religious services the pious light candles in the churches.

CHRISTMAS

In the countries of Central America—Costa Rica, El Salvador, Guatemala, Honduras, Nicaragua, and Panama—the majority of the Christian people are Roman Catholics. They follow in general the Christmas customs brought over from Spain by the conquistadors centuries ago. For the children, January 6, Three Kings' Day, is the time for receiving gifts (see Christmas customs in Spain, page 114, and in Puerto Rico, page 151). And as in Spain, the festival is marked by the ringing of church bells, the Mass at midnight on Christmas Eve, the gathering of families for the festival, and the making and enjoying of *nacimientos,* manger scenes.

In Central American countries, the manger scenes show a high degree of imagination and originality. Not only do they portray the Holy Family in the stable, the shepherds with their sheep on the hillside, and the Wise Men riding with their gifts, they also show a rich background of mountains, forests, and streams, sometimes against a painted background, sometimes in built-up scenes.

The children actively take part in making these manger scenes, which are set up in the homes, often on a table against the wall, and in the churches as well. The figures in the scenes are much beloved and are treasured from year to year. At midnight, in many places, the figure of the baby Jesus is laid in the manger, which has been empty until that time. During the Christmas festivities the children dance around the *nacimientos,* singing Christmas songs. The families visit from home to home to admire their neighbors' manger scenes. In Honduras, there is the custom of having *Posadas,* as in Mexico (see page 146).

Mexico

POSADAS

In the villages of Mexico, *Posadas*, literally "lodgings," are celebrated on nine successive evenings, beginning December 16. They dramatize the search of Joseph and Mary for a lodging in Bethlehem.

Mexican neighbors usually celebrate together and share expenses. Just as darkness falls, on the first evening of the *Posadas*, the children and adults, carrying lighted candles, form a procession and go through the village singing a litany. Usually one child carries a little platform on which are small figures of Joseph and Mary, with Mary usually riding a burro. Sometimes Joseph and Mary are represented by a man and woman or by a boy and girl. When the procession reaches the selected house, a leader knocks loudly on the door. Protests come from within that there is not room for them and they cannot enter. Then the person taking the part of Joseph sings, "I am Joseph. Take me in. I want a place for Mary to rest." After some discussion, permission is granted and finally the group enters the house and the little figures are placed in the crèche prepared for them. There are prayers and songs of rejoicing. More neighbors arrive and the ceremony becomes a party, with a feast, dancing, and perhaps a *piñata*.

The next evening the procession is repeated and the stop is made at another selected house, and so on throughout the nine days. (For words and music of *Posadas* songs see *The Whole World Singing*, Friendship Press.)

THE DAY OF THE HOLY KINGS

Santa Claus and Christmas trees are newcomers in Mexico and are becoming very popular symbols of Christmas, but the Day of the Holy Kings, January 6, has been celebrated ever since the Spanish people came to this continent, soon after Columbus discovered it. It is a family festival and is celebrated only where there are young children.

Usually the family puts its *nacimiento,* or manger scene, in a central place in the home, early in December. Generally the little figures are made of pottery and are old and beloved, though, of course, new ones are being made and bought each year. Children make new sheep of cardboard with wool or cotton glued on, and cows and donkeys to put into the scene. Fresh Spanish moss is added. The baby Jesus, *el Niño Dios,* or Baby God, as he is frequently called, is wrapped in freshly laundered swaddling clothes and laid in his tiny manger.

Every day the children look at the little figures and adore them, especially the doll that represents the baby Jesus. They visit their friends to see their *nacimientos,* and proudly show their own figurines when company comes.

Christmas comes and goes with celebrations of *Posadas* and Christmas parties. In Evangelical (Protestant) families there are programs in vacation school, in Sunday school, with special services in church and the singing of carols, plays, pageants, and recitations. Gifts are collected and given to the poor.

Christmas Eve dinner is served at a later and later hour as the children grow up. All the delicacies the family can afford are set forth— chicken, turkey, *mole* (meat with a rich spicy sauce), rice, soup, pasta, and beautiful salads. The special sweet is the *bunelo,* a very thin fluffy fried cake.

Decorations are carefully kept in place and every child looks forward to Twelfth Night after Christmas, the night of the Holy Kings or Wise

Men. Children are very, very good so that they will receive gifts. If the family has a manger scene, the children place their shoes in front of it. If there is a Christmas tree, the shoes are lined up under it.

Early, early in the morning there are squeals of delight as the children run to see what the Wise Men, who brought gifts of gold, frankincense, and myrrh to the baby Jesus, have brought to them.

This is the climax of the Christmas season for little Mexican boys and girls.—*Mrs. Ella H. Kepple*

Trinidad

CARNIVAL

Everyone in Trinidad grows feverishly excited as Carnival draws near—the last two days before Lent. For these two days, everyone forgets worries or troubles, poverty or hardship, and "plays carnival." All sections of the population—East Indians, Chinese, Creoles, Europeans—join in the celebrations, which somewhat resemble carnival festivities in other countries but which have special features of their own. One of these is the Trinidadian Carnival dance known as "jumping up." Another is the playing of the street bands and the singing of calypso songs composed for the occasion.

There is a special children's carnival held on the preceding Saturday, when prizes are given for the best costume worn by a child.

On the first day of the Carnival, everyone plays Old Masque, that is, they masquerade in their oldest clothes.

On the second day comes the playing of the bands and the dancing. Each band has its own wonderful costumes—pirates, robbers, dragons, or bats. They play road marches and dances, and sing new calypsos. The bands and the revelers in gorgeous costumes march by a stand where the girl who is chosen as Carnival queen stands crowned. Later comes the feasting, when each family delights in eating favorite foods.—*Constance Wagar* (See also pages 159 and 160.)

United States

THANKSGIVING

Thanksgiving Day in the United States falls on the fourth Thursday in November and is a national holiday, celebrated by people in all the fifty states.

The Pilgrims brought with them to New England the custom of keeping a Thanksgiving festival (see page 98), but gave it a special meaning and some special customs that have remained over the years. The Pilgrims celebrated their first Thanksgiving Day in their new country after their first harvest. They had come through trials and deprivations during their first year and now had gathered a bounteous harvest. They were filled with gratitude to God and with hope for the future, which they expressed in religious services. They held a Thanksgiving feast that lasted for three days and invited many friendly Indians to share it with them. The hunters brought in wild turkeys, geese, and ducks for the feast. The Indians brought deer. Bread was made of fresh barley and corn. There was fresh fruit. During the three days games were played, contests held with the Indians, and there was general merriment.

For some years Thanksgiving Day celebrations were confined to New England, but gradually the custom spread to other parts of the country. President Lincoln, in 1863, issued a proclamation for the first national observance of the holiday; and since that time presidents of the United States regularly issue Thanksgiving Proclamations.

Today the festival is celebrated as a time of family reunions and the traditional foods are roast turkey with cranberry sauce, fresh vegetables, one of which is usually squash, and probably pumpkin pie or apple pie for dessert.

Services of Thanksgiving are usually held in the churches, often a union service of a number of Protestant churches, through which gratitude is expressed for the good things that are enjoyed.

United States—Alaska (Eskimo)

CHRISTMAS

The largest Eskimo village is Point Barrow, with a population of about fifteen hundred, of which more than 90 per cent are Eskimos. The Presbyterian church at Point Barrow is the center of the social life of the village, practically all the families being associated with it.

Christmas is therefore a gala occasion in the church and has been for many years—the highlights being a church supper, served from 2 to 6 P.M., the Christmas tree and the gifts around it. Everyone in the village from the oldest grandparents to the youngest child is sure to be present.

The food is cooked in the homes and brought to the church by the families, each donating a share. One favorite dish is a soup made of caribou meat and rice. The young people of the congregation serve.

Until recent years, the presentation of the gifts came after the supper. But the pile of gifts became very large because the Eskimos brought their personal and family gifts to the church as well as others, and the distribution was very time consuming. Today, the gifts are presented the Sunday before Christmas and then only to the children.

After the supper comes the Christmas service, conducted in the Eskimo language, and the singing of carols.—From *World Family*

United States—Puerto Rico

FEAST OF THE CROSS

A typical festival celebrated in Puerto Rico is that in honor of the Holy Cross, *Fiesta de la Cruz*. This festival is held the last nine days of May. These *fiestas*, or parties, are celebrated by the singing of holy songs that tell about the crucifixion of our Lord Jesus Christ. They are held in outdoor amphitheaters, public parks, or in private homes.

On the stage of the outdoor theater a scene is prepared (hand-drawn or otherwise) in which the cross appears. This scene is decorated with flowers, colored paper, and branches of palm. On the first night of the *fiesta* a large box is placed on the stage. This box represents a stair. Each night thereafter another stair is added until there are nine. Men, women, and children sing in the choir the beautiful songs of the cross.

Each night a tray containing some refreshments and candy is sent to different families. They call these refreshments *capas*, "remembrances" or "souvenirs" of this festival. The family who receives the *capa* sends in exchange a gift of money, exceeding the worth of the gift sent. With the money that is returned, the host buys refreshments and candy for those present.

During the last night a big party is given, and after the singing of all of the holy songs of the nine days, everything is taken from the stage, and there is dancing and celebration.—*Edna S. Zech*

CHRISTMAS AND THREE KINGS' DAY

The Christmas celebration in Puerto Rico begins about one week before the twenty-fifth of December. During the week of the eighteenth, sleepers will often be awakened early in the morning by the singing of Spanish carols by a small group of young people and children passing through the streets of the town.

During this same week children go from door to door in the villages

singing carols to announce the news of the Magi. The children travel in groups of three and are dressed in bright-colored cotton costumes, usually red, lavender, and yellow, symbolic of kingly robes. On their heads they wear paper crowns on which are painted or pasted stars. Sometimes they wear masks to add to the distinctiveness of their costumes. In their hands they carry rhythm instruments, which they pluck or shake while singing. The children are very fond of singing and as long as someone is willing to listen, they do it heartily. Of course, they expect to be paid for their singing.

Two weeks before the sixth of January, tradition has it that three kings—by name Melchior, Gaspar, and Balthasar—start riding slowly toward Puerto Rico on their camels (some say horses) to visit the homes of all good children of the island. On the fifth of January, the eve of Three Kings' Day, *Día de los Reyes,* in every home the children gather green grass. Before he goes to sleep, each child places some grass in a box under his bed as food for the camels of the kings.

Sometime during the night of January 5, while the children sleep, the kings visit the homes, and in exchange for the grass place a toy, a bit of clothing, or some tasty food in the box under the bed.

Later in the morning, after church services, parties of young people go to the homes of their friends where they are treated to refreshments. Gay songs are sung, and a feeling of happiness prevails.—*Edna S. Zech*

GREETINGS OF NORTH AMERICA

In the morning	Good day
In the evening	Good evening
	Good night
On leaving	Good-bye
Christmas	Merry Christmas

Greetings in Spanish are given on page 167 and in European languages on page 118.

:6:

South America

FOLK FESTIVALS

Bolivia

LITTLE THINGS

Little Things, *Alacitas,* is the name of a fair held each October in Bolivia at which one can buy articles of miniature size. In the Bolivian markets one sees tiny chairs, tables, dolls, jewelry, houses, hats, all of fairy size.

Among the "little things" for sale there is a small clay man called Ekeko. He stands all of six inches high, and visitors to the fair hang on Ekeko's back the miniature articles bought during the day. There are tiny sacks of flour, rice, and macaroni, a gasoline can, a chair, and they are all on the same small scale as he. But he is magic! If you own an Ekeko, you will have an abundance during the year of each thing he carries.

So hasten and buy Ekeko and take him home! Anyone can buy him! Treat him very carefully, or good fortune will not be yours in the year ahead!

Ekeko is of Aymara Indian origin, and he dates back to the time of the Inca Empire, when the Indians held an annual fair in honor of their god of prosperity. Ekeko represents good fortune. On his head is the knitted cap of the Aymaras. He has a big head, a rotund abdomen, very short legs, long arms, and a happy expression on his face.—*Mrs. Murray S. Dickson*

THE RIBBONS

In Bolivia, when a baby gets his first head of hair, The Ribbons, *Las Cintas,* party is held for him. Each of his family's friends brings a bit of ribbon to the child. The festival is held among the Indian people and is more typical of the villages than of the towns and cities.

On his first birthday, the mother ties his hair up in tiny bunches with the ribbons he has been given. Then the family holds a big party to which the whole village is invited. At the party, baby sits like a king or queen. As all look on, each little bundle of hair is cut off close to the scalp. The friend whose ribbon is on the bundle gives in exchange for his ribbon (and its hair) a present or a gift of money for the baby. —*Mrs. Murray S. Dickson*

Ecuador

OLD YEAR

The whole family enters into the plans and preparation for the thrilling celebration of Old Year, *Año Viejo,* held in Ecuador on December 31. One will donate an old shirt, another a pair of pants, a hat, etc. These are stuffed with straw and sewed together to make the figure of an old man who represents the Old Year. Sometimes cypress branches are gathered into an arch over his chair, which is set up outdoors in front of the house. A pipe may go into his mouth, a cane in his hand. There the old man will sit, while the children dance gaily about him.

Inside the house someone will write his last will and testament, usually listing family faults that must go off with the old year. At midnight or before, if there are little ones who must go to bed early, the will of the old man is read aloud before the whole family, with much laughing and joking. Then the match is lit, and the old man goes up in flames, taking the family faults with him. Often someone will dress in black, as the old man's widow, and go around to the others begging for charity. Just at midnight the streets are filled with burning men and begging widows. After this comes the eating of the spiced food prepared for the occasion.

The typical New Year's dish is a crisp fried pastry made in the shape of a doughnut and dipped after cooking into a brown sugar syrup.—*Mrs. J. Benton Rhoades*

Peru

HARVEST FESTIVAL

At the time of harvest—in midwinter, since Peru lies below the equator—there is a festival of rejoicing. When the grain is ripe, the village people gather together to sing and dance. They have a special song that they sing, in which they act out the cutting of the grain with sickles, the gathering of the cut stalks into baskets, and the carrying home of the ripened harvest. (For words and music of the song, see *The Whole World Singing*, Friendship Press.)

MARKET DAY CELEBRATION

In the towns of the high Andes, Sunday is market day for the Indians of the surrounding areas. At daybreak the patter of their feet (the women move at a little run as if they could never catch up with all the things they have to do), and the clip-clop of the tiny hoofs of their burros can be heard in the streets as the sun is rising.

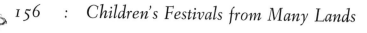

By the time the townfolk and tourists are up and about, the movable market is already in place. The street that was wide and bare the night before, now presents a colorful and exciting appearance. On both sides it is now a market, the goods for sale being laid out on mats along the curbs.

The objects for sale include useful household articles and some manufactured items; but for the most part they are goods produced by the Indians themselves. In one pile are beautiful llama wool blankets in harmonious shades and pleasant patterns, on one mat lie strings and strings of colored beads, on another little dishes of bright colored dyes. There will be hats, shirts, skirts, blouses, and coats hanging up so that they can be readily seen.

On one side of the street are clothes for women and girls and on the other apparel for men and boys. The women do the selling and they wear the traditional clothing of their particular people—a full black skirt, looped up in front to show an embroidered yellow or green or red underskirt, a bright-colored blouse of another shade, and a broad hat of black felt.

Candy, cool drinks, and pastries are sold by vendors along the market street. So the whole street presents the gayest sight imaginable.

Venezuela

BIRTHDAY PIÑATA

Venezuelan children, like most of their Latin American cousins, look forward to celebrating their birthday or "saint's day" with a *piñata* party. Many children are named after the saint whose name corresponds to the day on which they were born; so on a given "saint's day" all the little Rosas and Antonios in town may be celebrating their birthdays. In the morning they usually go to church to pay homage to their particular saint.

After *siesta* time in the afternoon the young guests, dressed in their best clothes and accompanied by one or more chaperones, begin to arrive, bringing gifts for the fortunate child. The center of attention at the party is the *piñata*. This is a receptacle, usually a pottery jar, filled with candy and perhaps other small favors, which is to be broken with a stick by the blindfolded children. (See also p. 132) The *piñata* may vary in size and elegance, according to the purse of the father. In the city it may be shaped and covered with crepe paper to represent a swan, a castle, or a ship. In the country areas it may be a large gourd or cardboard box decorated with a few paper streamers.

When all the guests have arrived and expectation is at a high pitch, the adult in charge leads the children toward the *piñata,* which is tied to one end of a rope that has been passed over the limb of a tree or some similar arrangement, to permit its being swiftly lowered and raised in pulley fashion.

The children are blindfolded and given the striking stick in turn, beginning with the smallest, who usually are unable to injure the *piñata,* dangling before their blindfolded eyes. As the larger children begin to take their turn at striking at the *piñata,* cracks may begin to appear in it, and the laughter and excitement increase. When finally the fatal stroke is dealt, the *piñata* breaks, and dozens of pieces of candy and small toys fall all over the ground. This is a signal for a wild scramble to see who can grab the most.

After the candy is shared and eaten, the refreshments are served. These vary according to the means of the family. In well-to-do homes it may be a big cake beautifully decorated; in poor homes it may be simply a drink made of water and cornmeal, seasoned with cinnamon. However costly or simple the *piñata* and the refreshments, the guests leave in a happy mood, wishing the guest of honor many more happy birthdays. The *piñata* party is popular also in Central American countries and Mexico.—*Mrs. John H. Sinclair*

CHRISTIAN FESTIVALS

Argentina

MAGI DAY

Magi Day is celebrated by Roman Catholics in Argentina and other parts of South America on the sixth day of January. On this day everybody remembers how the three Wise Men (who are believed to have been three kings) followed the star and arrived at Bethlehem to offer their gifts to the newborn babe. Popular tradition has connected this incident with the joy and happiness of children who on the night of the festival wait for the three legendary kings to come riding on their camels and to leave a gift in every little shoe. To make sure the kings know what to leave, the children often write them letters, which they place in the shoes before they go to bed. The children often leave hay and water for the camels of the kings.

What joy there is in the morning, when the children find in their shoes the gifts for which they asked, lovingly placed there (if they can possibly be afforded) by the parents during the night!

In the afternoon of January 6, the children gather with their friends and share the toys they were given, and at teatime they eat the traditional "Pie of the Magi." It is a cake, baked in the form of a ring and covered with sugar and jam, having little gifts in it.—*Sra. Luis Parrilla*

Bolivia

CARNIVAL

Carnival is celebrated in Bolivia and in other South American countries six weeks before Easter each year (just before Lent), and lasts for several days. On the first day of the festival the children dress up in their finery and are taken round and round the main square of their town, in cars and open trucks that are gaily decorated. From windows and balconies, friends shower the children with confetti and colored streamers.

The second and third days are devoted to eggshell throwing. The cooks in the homes have been saving the eggshells for months before the event. When breaking an egg for cooking, very little of the shell is removed and the insides of the eggs are shaken out of the small openings and the shells saved for carnival time. These are filled with flour or water and covered with a flour paste. Boys and girls get the prepared shells and go around the streets throwing them at one another. By night time, the participants are flour sprinkled and drenched with water, but very happy.—*May Turnbull*

CHRISTMAS

In Bolivia, Christmas, *Nochebuena,* is observed by putting up a crèche of *el niñito Jesús,* the baby Jesus. At the center of the crèche, which is usually banked by ferns, are figures of the baby, Mary and Joseph. Nearby are the Wise Men and their camels, the shepherds and their sheep. Around them are miniatures of the baby's pets and friends— burros, dogs, birds, fish, fowl, and people. Many of these tiny articles are bought at *Alacitas* (see page 153).—*Mrs. Murray S. Dickson*

Brazil

CARNIVAL

The most important festival in the large cities of Brazil is Carnival, which takes place the three days before Ash Wednesday preceding Lent. It is celebrated throughout Latin America, but in the large cities and particularly in Rio de Janeiro it reaches heights of extravagance that are noted the world over.

The festival is a very gay one and the people prepare for it for weeks. Everyone must have a special costume to wear, and even the very poor strive to have something for Carnival. During the festival the streets are full of merrymakers dressed as sailors, soldiers, historical characters, Indians, Pierrots (Little Peter, a jesting character dressed in white pantaloons and a large white jacket with big buttons), and so on. They carry small squirt guns containing perfumed water with which they douse others in the throng. Tons of colored confetti are thrown; and orchestras play constantly to provide music for the dancing that goes on, day and night. New songs are composed for the occasion and the best become popular.

One of the three days of Carnival is for the children who dress in their costumes and parade in the streets under the watchful eye of a grown-up member of the family. At the close of the three days everyone is weary and ready for the quiet of Lent.

SAINT JOHN'S DAY

Saint John's Day is one of the most important days of the year for the Roman Catholic children of Brazil. The celebration begins on the twenty-third of June, Saint John's Day, and continues until Saint Peter's Day on June 29. It is observed in all of Brazil but especially in the interior. (See also pages 98 and 142.)

According to a tradition of the Roman Catholic Church in Brazil,

Mary the mother of Jesus went to visit her cousin, Elizabeth, who promised to notify Mary of the birth of her child by building a bonfire in front of her house and by setting off fireworks. Thus on June 23, the day on which the birthday of John the Baptist is celebrated, almost all Catholic families in Brazil build large bonfires of pieces of dry wood, in front of their homes. Often they plant a tree, usually a banana tree, nearby.

The father lights the bonfire at six o'clock in the evening. All the family and friends gather around it, telling fortunes, singing, and dancing. Many unusual customs are a part of the observance of this day. One person may be seen jumping over the fire, while others may take off their shoes and walk over the coals when they are burned out, to prove that they have faith in Saint John and will not be burned.

When one person wants to be considered the special friend of another, both must walk around the fire three times, and each time they meet, each must say, "My friend, we are going to be comrades as Saint John commanded."

For the Saint John's Day feast, roasted corn and sweet potatoes and fresh hot coffee are prepared. The supper is generally served at midnight, but children may eat earlier. It consists of various types of food made with corn, such as *canjica,* made of green corn and coconut; *pamonha,* roasted corn, boiled corn; and *pé de moleque,* a kind of cake made with corn. During the remaining days of the festival the people do not make other bonfires, but they do eat the same kinds of foods and shoot off firecrackers.

In the special dances used during this festival, the

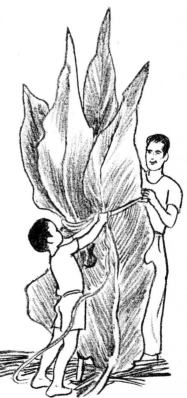

dancers dress like country people. The girls wear long full skirts of vivid colors, and ornament their hair with spangles, flowers, or ribbons. The boys wear long, patched trousers, colorful shirts with the tails out, brightly colored handkerchiefs about the neck, straw hats, and mustaches drawn on with charcoal.

The children take a very active part all through this family festival. The fireworks are especially for them. Many are beautiful and expensive. Shouts of joy fill the air as the boys and girls launch their large colorful paper balloons with candles inside, and watch them rise high into the air and make very bright lights before they quickly disappear. The fire balloons floating in the sky are the high point of the festival for the children, and they sing a song about them as they circle about the fire:

> Fall, fall, balloon!
> Fall, fall, balloon,
> Here in my hand.

—Told by Aretussa Pessoa to Miss Mary Garland Taylor

Chile

CHRISTMAS AND EASTER

In Chile, Christmas in the Evangelical homes is celebrated much as it is in the States. In the Roman Catholic homes, everybody goes to Midnight Mass on Christmas Eve and afterwards enjoys a big family dinner. Many have Christmas trees, for in southern Chile there is a strong German influence.

Easter is observed in an Evangelical community by special services during the week and communion service on Thursday. On Sunday the church is beautifully decorated with flowers, and there is special music.
—Miss Semeramis Kutz

DAY OF THE CROSS

May 3 is the Day of the Cross on the calendar of the saints. This day is celebrated by Roman Catholics in Chile as it was in olden times in Spain, when the poor went begging from door to door for food. It is a custom of the country and the village areas, not of the cities. In Chile, the Day of the Cross falls at harvest time, when the evenings are quite cold and generally rainy.

A cross about three feet high is made and covered with white flowers. Several friends or families gather in the evening at one home and go calling from house to house. One carries the cross, and at either side walks a person carrying a lighted white candle. Two others carry bags to receive the gifts of food. Not a word is spoken as the group of celebrants gathers outside a home where all join in singing, in chorus:

> Here comes the sainted cross,
> Visiting its devoted ones
> With a stub of a candle
> And a little jug of wine.

The door of the home is generally opened, and food, usually potatoes, onions, or fruit, is given and placed in the bags.

Then those outside sing again:

> Many thanks for the alms
> Which have been given.
> The Three Marias will come down to bless you.

If no food is given, the words are different:

> This is the home of the Keisers,
> Where live the stingy misers.

Sometimes twenty homes may be visited in one evening. At last the singers go to one of their homes and eat previously prepared food, such as cookies. The gift food is divided and taken home. Sometimes a group of children goes alone, but generally all ages are represented.—*Miss Semeramis Kutz*

Ecuador

CHRISTMAS

In the Evangelical mission, one whole day is devoted to the Christmas celebration to which the children of the Andean Indian families in the area are invited. During the morning, the older boys go to the woods and select a big tree. Meanwhile other children are busy making paper chains and decorations for it. By noon, the school patio is ready, with a beautifully decorated tree and a box of simple gifts under it. The children form a circle around the tree and present a program of recitations, songs, and folk dances. Then the gifts are given to each child. The parents also have a treat of some kind, candy, and perhaps a handkerchief, which are given at this time.

Then the preparations are begun for the evening program. All the parents and grandparents and uncles and aunts gather in the patio for this important event, the biggest of the year. Every child from first grade up has a part. Recitations, songs, dances, humorous skits, and last of all, the Christmas pageant, with Mary, Joseph, and the baby, and little black-haired angels. The evening ends with the singing of "Silent Night" and other carols.—*Mrs. J. Benton Rhoades*

DAY OF THE DEAD

Day of the Dead (*Día de los Muertos*) is a *fiesta* held in honor of dead loved ones by Indians of the Roman Catholic faith. Since there are no special celebrations for the children among the Indian people, the children must find their place in the *fiestas* of their parents. However, in this particular *fiesta,* held November 2, much of the excitement and anticipation lies in the preparations.

The day before the *fiesta,* every family in the entire community makes up a big batch of yeast dough. It is heavier and darker than our bread dough, but has a delicious flavor. Everyone in the household is allowed to knead the dough. At the proper time, it is divided into pieces and all go to work with it, using their artistic abilities. Some of the dough is colored and this is used in the decorations. Mummies, horses, clowns, soldiers, Indian women in embroidered blouses, are made. Competition runs high for the most beautiful creation. Then into the hot oven the dough figures go. Few families have ovens of their own, so the little figures are carried to be baked in a central oven which is rented by the hour. Meanwhile other delicious foods are being prepared at home—hominy and peas, parched corn, a blueberry sauce, and roasted guinea pig. Early the next morning, dressed in their finest, the family goes together to the cemetery. There a nice plateful of food is placed on the graves of the dead relatives, for their spirits to enjoy. While the parents talk, the children slip away and play their games, compare their bread dolls, and eat to their hearts' content. The dolls are dipped into the blueberry sauce before eating, to symbolize mourning.—*Mrs. J. Benton Rhoades*

Venezuela

CHRISTMAS

During the Christmas season in Venezuela, the *nacimiento,* or crèche, is placed in most of the windows or under the Christmas tree. The children of Evangelical families are busy learning poems, songs, and their parts in the dramas for the Christmas program at the churches, where gifts and candies are distributed at the close of the festivities.

All Venezuelans, young and old, gather around the table at midnight on Christmas Eve to eat their *hallacas* and green papaya preserves. The *hallaca,* which is uniquely Venezuelan, is a corn dough containing pieces of meat, olives, and other hot seasonings, wrapped in banana leaves and boiled, to make a kind of pie.

Many Venezuelan children still believe that the Christ Child brings their gifts, while others say the little mouse brings them. Gifts were formerly given only on January 6, the Day of the Three Kings, but now the exchange of presents often occurs on Christmas Day.—*Mrs. John H. Sinclair*

GREETINGS OF SOUTH AMERICA

Spanish is spoken in all countries of South America but Brazil and the Guianas, and in Central America, Mexico, and Puerto Rico as well.

Buenos días	Good morning
Buenas noches	Good night
Buenas tardes	Good afternoon
Hasta la vista	Good-bye
Hola	Hello or Hi
Feliz Navidad	Merry Christmas
Gracias	Thank you
Bienvenido	Welcome

GREETINGS IN PORTUGUESE
Spoken in Brazil

Bom dia	Good morning
Bôa tarde	Good afternoon
¿Como vai você?	How are you?
¿Vou bem, e você?	I am well, and you?
Obrigado	Thank you

: 7 :

Pacific Lands

FOLK FESTIVALS

New Zealand

MAORI POI CEREMONY

The Maori people are those who were living in New Zealand before the white men came. They are a handsome people, tall and strong. Gradually they are being assimilated into the rest of the population but some still cling to their old customs.

The Maori women and girls have a graceful kind of folk dance, done with balls, and called *poi,* which they used and still use to welcome visitors or to entertain at some other festival. They stand in a line, holding in each hand a flax fiber string about nine inches long, to the end of which is tied a ball of flax fibers or tightly packed dry leaves, sometimes painted. It is about the size of a tennis ball. A woman at the head of the line calls out the movements in a loud voice and the others follow her directions instantly. The balls are twisted up, down, to the right, to the left, overhand, underhand, forward, backward, and always in unison and in perfect rhythm.

The movements are graceful in the extreme and a delight to watch. They are supposed to represent the flight of butterflies, the soaring of birds, the swimming of fish, the gliding of canoes, and they are done to the soft music of a chant. The women and girls wear their long wavy hair loose, confined by flowers or a ribbon about their foreheads. For the dance the girls may wear *kiwi* feather cloaks or free-swinging skirts in gay colors.

Samoa

GREETING CEREMONY

The Samoans have a pretty ceremonial for greeting visitors and it is often the children who carry it out. They make flower chains, stringing the blossoms on long threads by means of needles, and then tying the ends of the threads together to make a wreath. The flower chains are called *ulas* and they are ceremoniously placed around the necks of visitors who are to be honored. There is a song about the making of the *ulas* entitled, "With Needle and Thread" which the grade school children in Hawaii and in Tutuila, American Samoa, sing when a big steamship from the United States brings tourists to their island home. (The music and words are to be found in *The Whole World Singing*, Friendship Press.)

Tonga

NEW YEAR

Perhaps because New Year, *Ta'u Fo'ou*, as it is called here in Tonga, comes to these "Down Under" islands during midsummer when the schools have their long holidays, it is a particularly happy time for children. On New Year's Day itself and for all the rest of the warm days of the first week of the year, the boys and girls form themselves into groups and go about from house to house serenading their families and friends. Some of them play harmonicas; others strum ukuleles or guitars; still others beat drums; and everybody sings.

As befits a new year, the songs they sing are all new, made up by the children themselves for the occasion. Some of them are hymns, thanking God for helping them through the problems of the past year, and some are songs of hope for the new year, and some are gay rounds.

When they have finished all the numbers in their little concert, the children move on to another house, but not before the householder who has enjoyed their music shows his appreciation by giving them fruit or cool drinks. Sometimes a particularly generous listener will give each performer a little woven mat or piece of tapa, the bark cloth that is made in the islands.—*Patricia Matheson*

CHRISTIAN FESTIVALS

Australia and New Zealand

CHRISTMAS

In Australia and New Zealand, Christmas comes at the height of summer and at school vacation time. This has a profound effect upon the celebrations, which are largely held out of doors. The Christmas greens used in decorations are flowers and sprays of bloom.

The Christmas dinner may be eaten outside the house in the warm open air, and the regular Christmas fare of roast beef, fowl, and pudding is enlivened by fresh vegetables, crisp salads, and newly picked fruits.

Christmas customs are much the same as in Europe and the United States, with toys for the children from Santa Claus or Father Christmas, family reunions, church services, and carol singing.

In Australia the people have a pleasant custom of going to the parks in the big cities and singing carols in the warm summer night. After the dinner the families may go to the beaches or the parks.

Tonga

SUNDAY SCHOOL DAY

As Tonga is a Protestant (Methodist) country, it is only natural that the most important church holiday should be one which is shared with Protestant children of many lands. This is Sunday School Day, known in Tonga as *Faka Me,* and celebrated on the first Sunday in May.

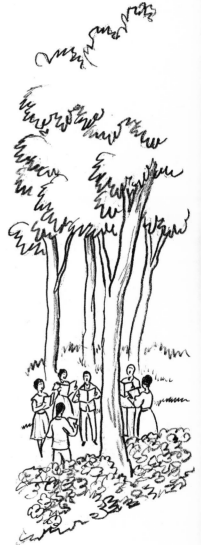

During the week preceding *Faka Me,* all the mothers have been busy sewing—for the girls new dresses, for the boys new *valas,* which are kiltlike skirts worn by boys instead of trousers. Bright and early on *Faka Me* morning, the children go down to the sea for their baths. Then they put on their new clothes and go to church. The sermon that day is preached especially for them, so they are all there.

As soon as the regular service is over, the *Faka Me* program begins. Even the little ones who have just learned to talk, stand up before the congregation and recite a verse or two of scripture or sing a hymn. The older boys and girls take part in Bible plays which they have made up or sing hymns to which they dance, using slow, solemn movements. Sometimes they even do a dance to the words of the Ten Commandments!

In Tonga, there is never a church service without a feast, and *Faka Me* is no exception. For the children, it is the most exciting feast of the year. Usually they have to wait until their parents and the older people have finished, but not on *Faka Me.* The children sit down first and the adults serve them. All the children of the Sunday school eat together. They do not sit at tables with knives and forks and spoons. Instead they sit on mats spread on the ground and eat with their fingers from long trays made of woven coconut fronds.

The trays, or *polas,* are piled high with all sorts of Polynesian foods—whole roast pigs, big lobsters in their red shells, chicken and fish steamed in coconut milk, yard-long potato-like vegetables called *ufi,* and all sorts of delicious fruits. The parents stand behind the children and fan them to keep them cool as they eat; and no matter how much a girl or boy eats, those mothers and fathers never say a word! For *Faka Me* is children's day.—*Patricia Matheson*

: 8 :

$\mathcal{F}$estival Time with Children

The material in the preceding chapters presents a rich portrayal of contemporary family life around the world. It pictures the families engaged in some of the most interesting and colorful of their activities—the celebrating of the folk and religious festivals which are dear to them. No matter where they live, what language they speak, what religion they profess, or what their skin color, people love to keep festivals. They treasure the customs traditionally connected with festivals and cling to them in spite of war, famine, fire, and flood. The disasters pass, the festivals remain.

All over the world festivals are held at certain seasons, such as the coming of spring, the ingathering of the harvest, the beginning of the new year, and celebrated by gay parades, singing, folk dancing, and feasting. The keeping of such festivals is an experience common to all mankind. These festivals strengthen and enrich family life and tradition and thus need to be recorded so children everywhere may enjoy and help to preserve them.

Parents, teachers, and leaders may make use of the

festival material in this book to promote understanding of the cultural heritage of other people, and through this understanding to encourage feelings of friendliness for them. This material may be used in the home, for community gatherings, and in public school or church school meetings of various kinds.

In the Home

Festivals being enjoyed in the home may be given added richness and variety by having the family learn about the keeping of a similar festival in another country or even by taking over some of its customs. At Christmas time, for example, the children may enjoy hearing how the festival is kept in the land of their forefathers; they may like to learn what happens at Christmas time in the land of a favorite book character; those who have French, Polish, or Spanish neighbors may want to read of Christmas customs celebrated in their homelands. The same interest and curiosity may extend to other seasons, such as Easter, Thanksgiving, or New Year.

In the Community

In neighborhoods where there is strong community feeling and where get-togethers are popular, this material on festivals may be the basis of one or more programs. A Thanksgiving program might take the form of a presentation of customs of the season as celebrated around the world. A Christmas program might be made up of a series of short skits or tableaux showing how Christmas is kept in many lands or in the countries of the chief national groups living in the community. A May Day festival would be popular for young people and children and it is one that lends itself well to community celebration. The program might include songs and folk dances, the making of flower wreathes, and even a maypole. Or there might be a special festival, such as a *piñata* party or Candy Holiday or a Feast of Lanterns (see pages 132, 156, 72, and 47).

In the Public Schools

The festivals described in this book may be used by public school teachers in connection with social studies or in relation to festival seasons that are celebrated in the classroom. A study of Africa, for example, may be enriched by having the children learn of the Leopard Pantomime or the Feasts of *Kapesi* and *Nganja;* and a study of Indian Americans may be made more interesting by hearing of the Bunny Dance, Green Corn or Maple Festival.

During the Saint Valentine's Day celebration in the classroom, the children may learn of the interesting origin of the festival and of the ways in which it is kept in other countries. The boys and girls may be encouraged to make May Day exciting and meaningful by giving May baskets to friends, as is done in parts of New England. The Thanksgiving and Christmas seasons may be made more colorful by the inclusion of some customs from other lands.

In the Church School

The church school is particularly interested in helping children recognize the common bond of friendship and understanding among the peoples of our interdependent world. The material on festivals may be used for special programs in the church school, such as Easter or Thanksgiving or Christmas, in connection with mission study themes, or as a part of a study in vacation church school groups. The descriptions of Christian festivals celebrated in other lands should have particular application to church school groups. The festival material may be used as part of the program for church family nights or to enrich the program at a school of missions. Along with resources from many other faiths, institutions, and agencies, this book seeks to develop both delight in celebration among families wherever they may live, and a sense of the worth and dignity of every person before God. The closing session of a vacation church school or of a mission study may be given added meaning by the presentation of festival customs in some of the following ways.

USING THE FESTIVALS

As Resource Material

In home, community, public school, or church school, the festival descriptions may be used to arouse interest, to supply information, and to increase understanding of the people and the countries concerned. Reports may be given about festival customs, pictures of them secured and examined (*The National Geographic Magazine* is a good source of pictures), parts of them dramatized, or made vivid through the use of puppets. Festivals may be enjoyed and participated in, just as games of a given country may be played with delight by our children.[1] A picture-story record of the festival customs may be made in notebooks or be displayed on bulletin boards. Or the children may be encouraged to make posters illustrating the festivals. Doll collections, often found in children's libraries or available through private collectors, may be studied for clothing details. The illustrations in this book, carefully researched for accuracy, should also be of great help in making such posters or drawings.

As Dramatic Material

Boys and girls may wish to present the information about festivals in the form of a simple drama, in order to make the festival come alive for their companions or for themselves. The preparation of such a drama could be one of the activities related to a study of regions of North America or of a foreign land, and its presentation could be one of the features of the final session which summarizes what has been learned.

[1] A companion book to *Children's Festivals from Many Lands* is *Children's Games from Many Lands,* by Nina Millen, Friendship Press, 1943.

Festivals which lend themselves to dramatic presentation are the following:

1. *Brother and Sister Day in India* (see page 53). The children may make and give gifts, as is done in India. Gifts may be made for older or younger brothers or sisters who are not part of the group and given to them as invited guests at a special program. Or the group may be divided into "adoptive" brothers and sisters and the giving be confined to friends. Simple and appropriate gifts for girls might be bracelets of woven colored threads or of colored ribbons, hair bows of ribbons, decorative pins made of small polished nuts glued to safety pins. Gifts for boys may be small bags of colored marbles, bags of nuts, or boxes of fudge or cookies.

2. *A "Little Things" Celebration in Bolivia* (see page 153). Connected with an interest in or study of Bolivia, the children may fashion little figures of clay or of soft wood, such as are made in that country to represent Ekeko, and attach to them bundles of miniature objects purchased at the dime store or shaped from clay or cut from paper.

3. *A Boys' Day and Girls' Day in Japan* (see pages 64 and 65). When studying Japan the boys in the group may dramatize the Boys' Festival in Japan, with banners cut from colored paper or from cardboard painted in bright colors, in the shape of a fish (carp), and hung from a post set up for the occasion. The girls may set up an interest center, using a series of shelves (pieces of wood set on upright bricks will suffice) covered with bright cloth on which they will place their best dolls and in front of which they will serve tea and cakes to their guests.

4. *A Gift Collection in Korea* (see page 67). Little cloth or paper sacks for collecting gifts, such as the boys and girls of Korea have on New Year's Day, may be featured in a Korea study. Instead of collecting gifts for themselves on the given day, the children may seek money gifts from their relatives and friends to be sent to the children of Korea (or some other place) as a gift from the group.

5. *Candy Festival in Turkey* (see page 72). The boys and girls may dramatize part of the Candy Festival, perhaps in connection with a classroom or community program or with a study of the Middle East (with emphasis on Turkey). A *Karagoz* show (shadow pictures) may be given; candy (perhaps Turkish *lokoum*) may be made, passed out on large trays to be enjoyed by the group and their friends; and large colored cotton handkerchiefs with a coin fastened in one corner may be tied to long poles.

6. *Old Year in Ecuador* (see page 154). Juniors may enjoy making an effigy of the old year and carrying on some of the customs connected with it in Ecuador.

As Out-of-Door Activities

An outdoor festival such as is enjoyed by children in any country in which there is a particular interest may become a group activity for spring, summer, or fall.

1. *A Kite Flying Outing in China, Korea, or India* (see pages 50, 67, and 55). A group of fourth- to sixth-grade children may make kites from colored paper, cut into fantastic shapes, and enjoy them on their outing. Make sure there is a wind that day, and choose a hilltop for this activity. A picnic lunch may be served when the kite flying is finished.

2. *A Maple Viewing or Flower Viewing in Japan* (an activity similar to a Moon Viewing, page 66). A group of children may go on a picnic to an outdoor spot where there are some fine maple trees or beautiful wild flowers. The finding of lovely leaves, nicely shaped trees, pretty wild flowers, and the sharing of these delights with the group may be part of the joyful experience. The teacher may tell how in Japan members of the group sometimes write short poems about the trees

or flowers to express their appreciation. Picnic lunches may be taken along in individual baskets as in Japan.

3. *A "Smell the Breezes" Walk in Egypt* (see page 21). A group studying about Egypt may plan a special walk of ten or fifteen minutes, during which they enjoy the fresh air and note natural beauties to talk about later. Or a whole session could be spent on the dramatization of this Egyptian festival by the children, with parents, brothers, and sisters taking part in a walk and a picnic.

4. *A Forest Picnic in Angola* (see page 17). A junior group studying Angola, or Africa in general, may use one of the forest festivals enjoyed by the African children as the inspiration for a special kind of picnic. The boys may bring the food, the girls the dishes and pans. In Africa, the boys would play games while the girls prepared the food, which all would then enjoy together.

5. *A Corn Roast in Brazil* (see page 161). A group meeting in late summer or early fall may have one of their meetings in the form of a corn roast, such as is held in Brazil on Saint John's Day. As they enjoy eating the roasted corn together, they may hear how boys and girls of Brazil participate in a corn roast in June when the green ears are ready for roasting. They may learn what other activities are part of the Saint John's Day celebration in Brazil.

As Seasonal Festivals

The children may celebrate one of the seasonal holidays of a country in which they are interested or about which they are studying, according to the customs there.

1. *New Year's Day.* Among the festivals in this book there are several different sets of customs for celebrating the New Year (see Index). One of the study sessions may be given over to enjoying a New Year holiday in the way that boys and girls would celebrate it in the country or countries being studied.

2. *Springtime Festivals.* If the study comes in the spring, the boys and girls may plan a springtime festival, according to the customs of the country in which they are interested.

3. *May Day Festival.* In parts of the United States, particularly in New England, the pretty custom of hanging baskets of flowers on a friend's door on May Day is followed (see page 133). The group may decide to give May Day baskets to their friends on this day, perhaps drawing from a basket the name of the friend to whom they will present the gifts. Or the group as a whole may decide to give May baskets to elderly people of their acquaintance, to sick friends, or shut-ins. The making of the May baskets should not interfere with the study going on but should be in addition to it or be one of the sharing activities connected with it.

4. *Midsummer Festival* (as in the Scandinavian countries, see page 91). If the study is being carried on in the summer, the boys and girls may have a celebration on Midsummer Day, June 24, following some or all of the customs that are carried on in Norway, Denmark, Sweden, and Finland. The celebration might be held just as darkness falls so that there could be a bonfire, with some games played around it and refreshments served as the flames die down. (See also Saint John's Festival, pages 98 and 142.)

5. *Harvest Festival* (see Index). A great many descriptions of the harvest festivals are contained in the book. Many churches celebrate the harvest season with a festival, and on such an occasion the children may well choose to portray a harvest festival that is enjoyed by the people in a particular country in which they are interested or about which they are studying.

6. *A Pageant of Festivals.* If a special program is desired—especially one that concerns itself with peoples of several different lands—a series of short dramatizations may be prepared, each one representative of some folk festival, enjoyed by families around the world. For example, such a

pageant of festivals might be appropriate for a community, county wide, or regional meeting; the closing session of a study; or a special meeting, using dramatizations or tableaux of the following:

A New Year Festival (see Index)
A Spring Festival (see Index)
A May Day Festival (see pages 89, 133)
A Midsummer Eve Festival (see page 91)
A Harvest Festival (see Index)
A Christmas Festival (see Index)

As Christian Festivals

Probably the most meaningful festivals for church group use are those that describe how familiar Christian festivals are celebrated in other lands and how they have been changed and adapted so that they will have significance for other peoples.

The descriptions of Christian festivals may be used in any number of different ways:

1. *As Resource Material in a Study.* In a study of Africa, India, Japan, or China, for example, information concerning the celebration of the Christian festivals by groups there may be presented.

2. *As Poster or Pictorial Material.* Posters or pictures may be drawn to show how one or two of the festivals are celebrated. The picture set *Children and Their Homes around the World* (Friendship Press) may be borrowed from the kindergarten or primary room and used as an example of such illustrations.

3. *As Dramatic Material.* Boys and girls may make one of their activities the dramatization of an Easter, Thanksgiving, or Christmas festival in the area of interest or study. The final program may include the presentation of the dramatization.[1]

[1] A helpful reference: *Let's Play a Story,* by Elizabeth Allstrom, Friendship Press, 1957.

4. *As Puppet Play or Dioramas*. Instead of presenting the festival custom through a dramatization, the children may make it into a puppet play or diorama.[1] The high point of the festival would be illustrated by the tableaux or dramatizations. These might include:

The Birds' Christmas in Sweden (see page 116)
A Christmas Game in Ethiopia (see page 30)
Christmas in South America (see Index)
Christmas in Pakistan (see page 80)
Christmas Lights in India (see page 75)

Adults as well as children may take part in the presentations and may enjoy the festivals together.

National Dress

The wearing of the national dress of a country is not necessary, though it does add to the color of the presentation. Space in this book does not allow for a description of festival clothing. Furthermore, in many countries, Western clothes are widely worn, although at festival times wearing of traditional clothing is customary. Illustrations in this book will help the group to know what type of traditional dress is worn in a country, and the clothing may be approximated. Children have vivid imaginations, and often a

[1] A helpful reference: *Here's How and When,* by Armilda B. Keiser, Friendship Press, 1952.

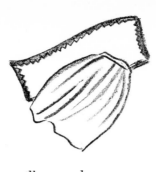

headdress, a shawl, a belt, or jewelry will serve them as a satisfactory "costume."[1]

Food

Space also precludes the description of various foods used at festival time. Again the leader may seek to improvise food that will be approximations. Fritos may be served to approximate Mexican food and some South American food. Rice cakes will serve as a form of Chinese, Japanese, and Korean food. *Lokoum,* a Turkish sweet, is typical of Middle Eastern sweets. Foreign food bakeshops or restaurants can sometimes supply the desired festival food.

If the leader has access to the series of *Fun and Festival* books, published by Friendship Press, descriptions of various kinds of food will be found therein.[2]

Greetings

A number of greetings used in various lands are included in this book. Knowing the greetings commonly used among a people is one way of becoming acquainted with them. The exchange of greetings is also a simple form of dramatization and one that children can easily carry out.

[1] It should be pointed out that guests in the United States at embassies, the United Nations, and elsewhere, prefer not to have their traditional clothing referred to as a "costume." This word is more appropriate in connection with Hallowe'en, masked balls, and the like.

[2] The *Fun and Festival* series includes Africa, India, Pakistan, Ceylon, Nepal, Japan, Latin America, the Middle East, the Rim of East Asia, Southeast Asia, and the United States and Canada.

The greetings given here may be used during a study of any country. Leaders and children may greet each other at the start of each session with the common form of greeting in that country.

A short dramatization may be worked out for a special program, using a number of the greetings from various countries, and may include:

An African Greeting (see page 40)
A Spanish Greeting (see page 167)
A *Namaste* from India (see page 86)
A Japanese Greeting (see page 87)
A French Greeting (see page 119)

Index

A WORD ABOUT THE FORMAT

The text of this book is set in linotype Fairfield, the first type face from the hand of the distinguished American artist and engraver, Rudolph Ruzicka.

COMPOSITION BY: WESTCOTT & THOMSON, INC.,
PHILADELPHIA, PA.

OFFSET LITHOGRAPHY BY: AFFILIATED LITHOGRAPHERS,
INC., NEW YORK

BINDING BY: H. WOLFF BOOK MANUFACTURING COMPANY,
INC., NEW YORK

JACKETS AND COVERS BY: AFFILIATED LITHOGRAPHERS,
INC., NEW YORK

TEXT PAPER: CRESTOPAKE TEXT VELLUM FINISH

Typographic design: Margery W. Smith

Binding design: Louise E. Jefferson

DISCARD